RUNNING FREE
SEBASTIAN COE
with David Miller

SIDGWICK & JACKSON
LONDON

First published in Great Britain in 1981 by
Sidgwick and Jackson Limited

First paperback edition 1982 (revised and updated)

The authors wish to thank the *Daily Express,
The Guardian, The Sunday Telegraph, The Times,
Athletics Weekly* and *Sports Illustrated*
for permission to reproduce extracts and to draw
upon original material. We also wish to express our
gratitude to our families, for patience, support
and enthusiasm given in many ways; likewise to close
friends of Sebastian's. We just managed to meet the
publishers' deadlines with unstinting assistance and
advice from Marita Miller in the organization and
typing of the text – of which Libby Joy was a
sympathetic editor.

ISBN 0-283-98857-6

Typeset by Fleet Graphics, Enfield, Middx
and printed in Great Britain by
© ollins, Glasgow
for Sidgwick and Jackson Limited
1 Tavistock Chambers, Bloomsbury Way,
London WC1A 2SG

British Library C.I.P.

Coe, Sebastian

Running Free.
1. Coe, Sebastian
2. Runners (Sports) – England – Biography
I. Title II. Miller, David, *1935 Mar. I* –
796.4'26'0924   GV697.C6/

ISBN 0-283-98857-6

For Peter . . . or was it Percy?

Foreword

by Mary Peters, M.B.E.

(1972 Olympic Women's Pentathlon Gold Medallist
and now British Women's Athletics Team Manager)

The first time I watched Sebastian Coe competing was at an indoor meeting at Cosford some years ago. I don't recall if he won, but I remember saying to his father Peter, 'Seb will be the pride of British Athletics in the future'. Little did I realize how soon Seb would be exciting huge crowds all over Europe.

Since Roger Bannister broke the four-minute mile in 1954, there have been many notable British middle distance runners – Ibbotson, Simpson, Whetton, Stewart, Foster. But none has caused the same excitement as Seb did in the 'Race of the Century': the 1,500 metres battle between Steve Ovett and Seb, with its 'preview', the 800 metres. The world waited expectantly for their Moscow Olympic meetings.

I was on Village duty and sorry not to be able to see the 800 metres final live. Many of us considered Seb had the speed and style to win, but as Steve broke the tape those of us watching on television stood in stunned silence. Thrilled as we were by more gold and silver medals, we had felt the gold was meant for Seb.

I waited at the Village gate for his return, knowing his disappointment. He blamed no one but himself, yet he proved his ability and character by fighting back to win the 1,500 metres. That took guts. I almost could not bear to watch the final, but it was a beautifully judged victory.

Seb has met success and failure and remains unassuming. He will inspire youngsters for years to come to share the fitness, exhilaration and friendship which sport provides.

Illustrations

Contents

Introduction

Nice guys finish last, they say. This is the story of a young man who had the pulse of almost a whole sporting nation quickening for him because he personified so many of the aspirations of the anonymous. To millions, he was the quiet boy next door with the kind smile, a universally favourite son whose personal odyssey reached out and touched the soul of a nation down on its luck and drained of self-esteem. The fascination was as much whether a seemingly frail student might win a 1,500 metres foot race for Britain and raise the Union Jack in odious Russia, as the more fundamental human issue of whether virtue would triumph over largely self-inflicted adversity. If sport is a microcosm of life, then the events of the 1980 Olympic Games in Moscow were as turbulent as any medieval epoch. In reality, he was anything but the boy next door.

This is also, essentially, the story of a family, and of the father and son in particular: an ordinary English family who have managed not to take upon themselves false mantles because one of their four children became, in the space of a year, as well known a face on the television screen as the Prime Minister. It is the family ethic, too, which has helped endear him to the people at a time when the decline of the family, and of trust and respect between parents and children, is contributing to debility in the Western world.

While Soviet and East German medals are heralded by their leaders as being symbolic of the supremacy of the mother state, it did not pass notice that in the gaining of many of Britain's medals there was an element of family achievement. Not only was there Sebastian Coe and his father Peter – his coach and constant companion – but Allan Wells and his altruistic wife Margot. There was also Sebastian's great rival Steve Ovett and his ever attentive mother Gay, while Daley Thompson acknowledged his debt to his Auntie Doreen, who had nurtured him since he was a child and was there in Moscow cheering. Gary Oakes, unexpected bronze medallist, owed much to his father, a north London coalman. Swimmer Sharon Davies was coached by her father, and Duncan Goodhew walked to the start wearing a cap belonging to the father who sadly did not live to see his son's triumph.

This book attempts to portray the quite remarkable relationship between an athlete and his father at the ultimate level of performance. Sebastian is singular because, in spite of his athletic excellence, he is adamant that this esoteric excellence should not dominate his life. His existence beyond the red ribbon of track in front of him is even more important than the medal at the finishing line: an attitude which, when coupled with an intense desire to be one of the greatest athletes in history, requires a very disciplined dedication. His medals and his many records are the rewards of a brutal self-discipline largely unknown, or forgotten, in today's indulgent, insecure society.

I am aware that I run the risk of making Seb seem unrealistically a paragon, that I may stand accused of sycophantic prejudice; but the fact is that not only did heredity, the genetic accident of birth, grace him with unique physical and physiological attributes, but they are found in conjunction with an upbringing of love and application which has produced in him a serenity and an equanimity which I have observed in few world-famous sportsmen. He has adjusted to the burden of being taken for granted as public property with the patience of Job. Over recent years of mounting pressure and tension, I have waited for the moment when he might snap, but it has never come. While he has an absolute conviction in his spectacular ability, he is without conceit. Only once have I seen him even reproachful, and during the days of the most searching inner crisis an athlete can ever have had to endure, he unfalteringly exhibited a disarming outward calm. What the result of suppressing his feelings might have been had they not been gloriously released on the track we shall never know. He merely said: 'I never want to feel again what I felt after the 800 metres.'

The seed for this book was planted, I suppose, when I first went to interview an up and coming young athlete at Loughborough University shortly before his first international success in March 1977. A shy, dark-haired twenty-year-old came through the swing doors of the poshest pub in town, and over 'steak and two veg' and spotted-dog pudding, modestly explained how he was aiming to 'peak' for the Moscow Olympics on the absurdly low training mileage of thirty-five miles a week.

He thought he might one day specialize in the 5,000 metres, in which an 800 metres potential 'of hopefully 1 minute 45 seconds' would be useful. Little did either of us know – though perhaps, on second thoughts, he had an inkling – that in just over two years he would shatter that 1:45 'potential' and, with it, the 800 metres world record, and that by 1981 he would achieve a remarkable eight world records, with still no sign of a limit. What was apparent in 1977 was his crisp, clear view of his objectives, and a rational assessment of his own particular qualities which somehow made you sit forward on the edge of your chair and forget you had a train back to London to catch. When, a few days later, running blisteringly from the front, he won the European Indoor 800 metres, with a time a fraction outside the world indoor record, I wrote in the *Daily Express*:

'The boy – for physically that is almost what he still is at twenty – who ran away with the European Indoor title in San Sebastian is about to pick up the torch where Brendan Foster put it down after Montreal. The stage is ready for a duel which will give athletics a kind of spectacle it has not had since the days of Bannister, Chataway, Pirie, and Ibbotson – between the quiet-spoken Coe and confident, extrovert Steve Ovett. Both these gifted but vastly different young runners are capable of getting close to, if not beating, world record times for 800 or 1,500 metres. Coe reckons he may ultimately move up to 5,000 metres. Yet they are still three years or so off their peak, which will optimistically coincide with the Moscow Olympics. Their personal rivalry, as yet unfurled, should be as great a spur as any medal. Ovett, so disappointing in Montreal when he misjudged his tactics in the outside lane of the 800 metres final, has spent the winter ploughing through the mud of cross-country runs. Coe, inwardly confident but as modest as Ovett tends to be brash, has been working at basic speed with spectacular results. There is no question that Ovett has one of the most superb physiques of any middle distance runner in the world, with untold strength. But Coe has shown, by going to the front in San Sebastian after 200 metres and staying there, that his relatively light body conceals enormous reservoirs of power. It is sad that almost by definition Olympic champions must be

13

odd-birds and loners. Coe at the moment appears to be madly normal. We shall wait and see what a summer in the limelight will do to him, but I fancy he is heat resistant.'

What now began to catch the public's eye was a runner who was like no runner they had seen before. While Ovett, who had matured earlier, exuded power in the manner of Montreal Olympic champion John Walker of New Zealand, Coe's running gave an ethereal sensation that he was floating. He was in the race but somehow apart from it, and every time he ran there was an aura of destiny. 'Effortless power' is a cliché of my trade but if ever an athlete possessed it, here it was. When I was eighteen, and a modest junior sprinter, I had competed in the August Bank Holiday British Games at the White City, and had been overawed to be warming up on the centre of the track at the same time as an athlete whom I revered, the twice Olympic 800 metres champion Mal Whitfield of the United States. For twenty-four years I regarded Whitfield as the supreme stylist, a beautifully relaxed runner who changed pace so imperceptibly that spectators and rivals alike could measure the change only by the gap which opened. Now, here was the flowing gracefulness in a British runner. Moreover, the set of his head upon his shoulders and the cadence of his limbs imparted an aesthetic quality which further aroused the public's acclaim. In the moment of his triumph in Moscow the *New Statesman* would refer to him – without exaggeration – as the Nureyev of the track. It was that cadence for which Peter Coe had been striving throughout the twelve years and thousands of hours of training. The father's achievement in navigating his son from fourteen-year-old wraith to Olympic champion and world record breaker is a coaching phenomenon probably without parallel in the history of sport. It is a partnership in which their own curiosity is as much a force as ambition.

Part of the understanding I struck up with Seb, even though he is young enough to be my son, stemmed from the fact of our mutual experiences, sometimes amusing, of having enthusiastic, mildly eccentric fathers from a patriarchal, almost Victorian-London background. In spite of having little initial knowledge of the sport, but proffering substantial encouragement, my father was largely instrumental in my reaching the fringe of the 1956 Olympic soccer team, and I became intrigued by the inter-action between Seb and his father even when the son had reached such a

14

peak of proficiency: a synthesis of mutual pride and ambition.

When he was fifteen and was asked by Angela, his mother, what would happen if he did not achieve what he wanted in athletics, Seb had replied simply that he would find a sport at which he *could* succeed. Privately he had been motivated by the example of Jonah Barrington who, when a near alcoholic at Trinity College, Dublin, had determined to make himself into world squash champion within two years, even though he could hardly play the game. The difference for Seb, of course, was that he was already highly proficient at something.

Early in 1979 I had discussions with Sidgwick and Jackson about the possibility of writing a book on the Moscow Olympics, and when it was discovered that they had had the idea of a book about Sebastian Coe it was natural that the two should be merged. Subsequently Seb achieved in 1979 the sensational coup of three world records in forty-one days, and another four in a, literally, blistering summer in 1981. This book is neither a biography nor an autobiography – for, as Seb would insist, his life still lies ahead – but is an account of one athlete's quest for success.

The success has not only earned him fame, about which he remains equivocal, but affection on an unprecedented scale, from young and old alike, and from many who would normally take scant interest in sport. It is probable that he is our most popular sportsman since Henry Cooper and Bobby Charlton were in their prime. He was voted sportsman of the year by wide margins by the Sports Writers' Association of Great Britain in three successive years from 1979 to 1981, the first sportsman ever to be so. After winning the 1,500 metres in Moscow he received more than 4,000 telegrams, letters, and cards of congratulation and good wishes, many of them sent anonymously by humble people not seeking, however distantly, to associate themselves with the achievement but to express appreciation of it: 'Three Brits in Paris', 'Two admirers in Bristol', 'All the girls on the telephone exchange at Harlow'; and so on, endlessly. From school children to retired nurses living alone with their cats came the common message of shared happiness. Over two months after the race, 10 October was the first day on which the post brought nothing. Of course it is unhealthy for people to sublimate their lives too far to the sporting exploits of others, as happens in our great football cities. But between 1979 and 1981 Sebastian Coe gave to others an

15

elixir, that hope of better things which famous deeds give us to draw upon freely.

Not that he was aware of all this in Moscow, where he was conscious only of his daunting test of nerve and character. It was later that he admitted: 'It never sank in at the time what it would mean if I lost the 1,500 metres. Not even in the darkest moments after the 800 metres did it concern me how it might affect others. It was a week or so later, suddenly, when I was out training at home, that I broke into a cold sweat with the realization of what I had been carrying in terms of public goodwill, of the years of effort put in by family and friends, and it was a little frightening.'

Ironically, the same factor which placed tremendous pressure upon him simultaneously gave him the nerve to survive that pressure: the belief, shared with only a few and, for a while afterwards, still doubted by some, that he had the ability, the sheer unrivalled class, to win both races in Moscow whatever way they were run. I believed it then and now, yet, because of his defeat in the 800 metres, the ultimate proof of his supremacy was still to come. A year later it did. Such was his confidence that he had even said before the Games, in answer to those who questioned his stamina, that he would like the heats, the semi-finals and the final of the 1,500 metres to be run all on the same day, 'and then let's see what happens'.

We know what *did* happen – and that within a twelvemonth he had unleashed a tornado of calculated record-breaking the like of which may never be seen again. Such was the focus of the nation's attention on his rivalry with Ovett that BBC television stopped the 'Nine O'Clock News' to relay from Brussels the astonishing climax to that Golden Summer . . .

January, 1982   DAVID MILLER

Publisher's Note

To differentiate between the authors, text by
Sebastian Coe appears within bold quotation marks

1: Beginnings

❝ Some of my earliest recollections are of running. Looking back it seems that from the time I could walk I preferred to run. It just seemed natural. When I was still quite young we moved from London to Stratford-on-Avon because of my father's work. We lived on the edge of the town and I would regularly run two miles or so into town and back again on errands for my mother, never using a bicycle, preferring the feeling of running. I can remember jogging beside my sister Miranda's pram, which must have been when I was no more than three. When we went for picnics in the Cotswolds, I would open and close the gates and then run behind the car. I never walked anywhere, it seems. I had a genuine, instinctive love of running, so that even between the ages of twelve and seventeen, when the rewards of training were not always immediate or tangible, self-motivation was never a problem. In becoming my coach my father made sacrifices, of course, though he never really voiced them. It is impossible to know by how much he might have advanced his engineering career had he not devoted the time he has to my coaching. Yet I have made my own sacrifices, as every runner does – training in the morning, then the gym at lunchtime, training again in the late afternoon, all fitted around the business of keeping an academic programme up to scratch. The evening comes and you'd like to go out, but you are just too tired. As Brendan Foster has said, 'running is just feeling tired all the time'. There are days when walking round a department store, or even walking up stairs, can almost kill you. When I spent the winter before the Olympics living and training outside Rome, staying with friends, the public, had they known where I was, would have had visions of *la dolce vita*. How wrong they would have been! The reality was falling asleep in a chair in the evening, knowing that Rome, with all it had to offer, was twenty minutes down the road, while I was slumped there, often alone – me and the BBC world service! ❞

Sebastian Newbold Coe was born in Chiswick, West London on 29 September, 1956, the autumn during which the celebrated Russian ballerina Ulanova was enrapturing audiences at Covent Garden, and Peter Coe had returned to England from business in America specially so that his first child should be born at home. The threads of heredity and environment which would ultimately, on a sunny afternoon in Moscow, lead to the most coveted honour an athlete can win, were coloured as much by artistic inheritance and influence as robust physical endowments.

His mother, Angela, had been an enthusiastic repertory actress before her marriage. Angela's own connection with ballet and theatre would inevitably have some physical significance for the children − her own mother had danced with the legendary Pavlova, and Seb's sister would become a ballet dancer. If you could not write, paint, or dance in her family you were unusual. When Angela married Peter Coe, who had diligently and extensively qualified himself as a production engineer, there was some surprise among the family; engineering to many people still had overtones of oil rather than the drawing-board. The designing of industrial machinery was one of those areas unknown to vast numbers of the British middle-class, whose educational prejudice in favour of the arts has so shaped and limited Britain's industrial status in the second half of the twentieth century. (As for running, that was something one occasionally did to keep healthy.)

❛My mother's mother, who is half Irish and half Welsh, was the daughter of an artist who was an R.A., and she herself had to give up dancing when she broke an ankle. On my father's side, his grandfather, Robert Coe, was a sprinter from Sunderland in his youth, competing against the north-east professionals, 'so fast he could kick over a rabbit' they used to say. But his son Percy, my grandfather, was never a sportsman, suffering for a long time from a bad leg. He was a small business-man, a carpenter-shopfitter, who worked a lot in Regent Street, and lived until he was seventy-three. My father's mother was the daughter of Harry Newbold, something of an eccentric, who was born with a silver spoon in his mouth and was sent to boarding school in Scotland when his parents died young. He was an engineer who was also involved in the circus and the vaudeville stage. He knew

Chaplin, and was still roller-skating when he was eighty-two. Before she married Percy Coe my grandmother had often had to stay with her grandparents in Walkley, then a village on the moors just outside Sheffield, when her parents were on tour. Today, ironically, Walkley is only half a mile from our house within the city itself. **)**

Violet, Peter's mother, is the personification of the London which endured the Blitz, of the Flanagan and Allen line, 'Who do you think you are, Mr Hitler?' If Seb's equanimity comes from his mother, and in turn, quite probably, from her father, it is easy to see where the Churchillian resolve which lifted his spirit in Moscow came from. Granny Violet has that kind but firm demeanour which would have seen Rommel off with an umbrella. At an international at Crystal Palace, she was the only person in the grandstand to remain seated during the German national anthem. Her son is also slightly formidable. Peter, a tall, slim man who was a more than competent club racing cyclist in his younger days, is unquestionably an authoritarian. When peering over or through his dark-rimmed glasses he bears more than a passing resemblance to the cartoonist Giles's schoolmaster, Old Chalky. Yet behind the austere exterior beats a sensitive heart. Unerringly, he knew his own son, who – like many small boys – had something of the appearance of a young giraffe in the early days. He would need the most careful, sensitive coaching.

'He was a very nervous young boy, he suffered from nervous eczema as well as pollen asthma. He was incredibly sensitive. He was deeply shocked when he failed his 11-plus, but as always I gave it to him straight, saying, "you can either be a Secondary Mod drop-out, or get down to it and get your 'O' levels". He grafted and grafted, and got eight 'O' levels. He was, I think, the only one of the four children who would let me stand behind him and shove. He always had an ability to get the maximum out of what he's got.'

The outsider might wonder whether Peter was disposed to propel Seb more than he might have done for the very reason that his pushing was accepted. He was, one senses, disappointed when slim, feline Miranda, who was with the Royal Ballet and then the

21

Ballet Rambert, ultimately gave up ballet to become a cabaret dancer in Las Vegas, subsequently switching to modelling in New York, and then back to cabaret in Reno. Nicholas, the family wit and court-jester, had the makings of an outstanding competitive cyclist, until he suffered a cycling accident while doing a paper round and thereafter never put his undoubtedly fine physique to the test again. He is now the young-man-about-town in London. Emma, the youngest – now studying design, forever laughing infectiously, often at herself – gives you the impression she would love to be pushed but is not quite sure where to. Binding the house together is Angela, self-effacing, patient counsellor to all five others, the soft pedal subtly shaping her husband's cadenza.

Theirs is a happy, solid, busy, rambling household up on a hill beside Sheffield University, the rear view overlooking a large university recreation area directly below the garden, where Seb has done much of his laborious repetitive sprint training. The city lies a few minutes down the hill and in the other direction, equally close, is the vastness of the Derbyshire Peak District, spreading across the Pennines. There, runner and coach have painstakingly welded their remarkable, enduring partnership. Peter says:

'Until a few years ago I drove both of us hard, patience was not my virtue. I expected him to be ready on the dot for training! But he was a splendid fellow, he knew better how to live with me than anyone in the family. He learned obedience, yet by the time he grew up his father wasn't God, he knew that I had feet of clay. We worked on a programme and he never badgered me or questioned the programme. At fourteen I knew he was good, at sixteen I felt a strange kind of certainty that if I was patient I had a world beater. At that time we could not be sure of the distance and would probably have said 5,000 metres, but already he was veering towards the 1,500 metres.'

❛ I remember arriving at Tapton School in Sheffield halfway through an academic year, also the strangeness of being in a big city for the first time, and playing nothing but soccer. In my first game I played madly for an hour, rushing all over the place trying to tackle everyone to prove myself with the bigger boys. The master in charge was John O'Keefe, I thought he was terrific and I wanted to be able to play like him. He was a bit like the master in the film *Kes*, only John didn't show off like him. John was very good to me and it was with him that I stayed out in Rome – he moved there to an English school some time ago. Failing the 11-plus was one of the best things that happened to me. Going to Tapton, a big-city school, I found a large social mix; it was a very good school within the state system, a sort of 'people's Eton'. It was tough, and more character-building than a small grammar school would have been. Some of those I knew when we lived in Stratford who went to the grammar school have done less well academically than many of those at Tapton. We were a form of 'failed 11-plus', yet many have come through and had university educations, getting degrees. Of my five best friends, all emphatic failures at eleven, one got a first in physics at Sheffield, another a first in maths at Warwick, and two got degrees in English at Liverpool. We came through as fighters.

Peter always has an unbending attitude to my academic side as well as to my running, and if athletics hadn't been able to become an academic thing with him, almost intellectual, he wouldn't have been so interested. He was never one for the gossip and the old wives' tales of the sport, and I suppose that attitude has rubbed off on me. I would be very surprised, as far as he is concerned, if his attitude didn't contain an element of wanting to produce something just for the hell of it – in a totally natural way – pushing potential into new areas. When people have said to him in the past, 'You've let it become an intellectual exercise', his answer was, 'you're dead right!' I couldn't have asked more from him. Being an engineer he was good at maths, but didn't know much about statistics. In order to be able to help me with my Statistics 'A' level he enrolled two nights a week as a mature student at a local college. I can't think that I would do that for any of my kids. But if that seems too serious, taking things too far, he retained a balance. When I was fifteen, we went over to Stretford, for a league race, and when we got back home late there was no time left for revision for a CSE paper the next day. (I had to do both CSE and 'O' level.) I said, 'that's the end of my CSE!' but Peter merely said, 'you're better off with the 1:56 for the 800 metres which you got this afternoon'. In the event I got both.

He was always particularly good when it came to injuries, insisting we treat them with the utmost respect, and that I should never run through them as some people do. When we were out on

23

runs on the moors when I was young, he would take me down the long, steep inclines by car, so that I should not damage the bones while they were still growing, and then make me work uphill where the stress is only on the muscles. It is when things go wrong that a good coach is priceless. I always remember what David Hemery said at a coaching course for schoolboys: 'You're all going to get injuries and the true worth of an athlete will always come to the fore when he is injured.' Two weeks later I found I had stress fractures of the shins in spite of Peter's caution, and was out of competition for a year – a very trying year. **)**

It would be difficult to over-estimate the contribution made by Angela to Seb's ascent of Olympian heights. She has been strong without being too demonstrative, supporting without being fussy, influential without interfering, bringing to the intensity of a situation the soothing ministrations of a mother and a wife. Throughout the arduous years in which the man and the boy were continually driving towards a distant and not always clearly defined objective, she was able to hold the emotional tiller as they negotiated rapids which at various times could have capsized one or both of them.

'I suppose I first realized how serious Seb was when we came to Sheffield and, at the age of twelve, he joined Hallamshire Harriers. For a long time I thought Peter was going barmy over someone who wasn't going to be exceptional. I was amazed that Seb never complained at the routine, at the sheer pain in his hands from the cold when he came back from training sometimes in mid-winter up on the hills, when he was told how many hours' sleep he had to have! He had a wide circle of friends, yet he willingly opted out of social events. At his 'O' level stage I felt it was very much in the balance whether he continued. Even Christmas Day had a timetable, including training and, say, two hours' geography revision. I can remember Peter saying, ''you can do it, one helps the other''. Seb managed it all, and the same with 'A' levels, his self-discipline was astonishing. There were times in the early days when I wished, I suppose, that he wasn't so good at running. Sports days were embarrassing and I'd find myself thinking, ''*please* lose something''. You could hear other mothers muttering, ''it's only

24

going to be Coe again, I don't know why we bother to come". For years I accepted Peter's saying, "he's going to be world class" while I was tending to think to myself, "I just hope it doesn't blow up in his face". I didn't want either of them to be disappointed. Because I saw less of what was happening up there on the hills, I suppose I probably had less faith in the ultimate success.'

❝ In some respects you could say my mother has been even more important in helping towards what I've done than Peter; not down on the track or working out my training schedules, but in providing a solid base for everyone in the house, in maintaining an air of consistency and continuity. For every extra training session, for every extra race, it means a whole day reorganized in terms of meals and laundry and so on. My mother is very level-headed, very easy going, and has a sense of humour, which as far as I am concerned is more important than anything. She has cushioned us against a lot of the anxieties, although athletics itself is marvellous for releasing pent up feelings. People say never play cards with a really successful sportsman because they have to win whatever they are doing. But these days I can never be bothered to be aggressive about anything *outside* athletics, and my aggression on the track is all inside. It was different when I was younger. Miranda and Nick say that when I was eight or nine I used to throw down the bat if I was out when I was playing cricket or claim it was the wind which had taken off the bails. I was very nervous for at least three days before a race in school events. But learning to control athletic nerves helped control exam nerves eventually. I threw away the 11-plus, but now I can sleep without problem the night before a big race or examinations. ❞

One of his early reports at Tapton, for French lessons, records that 'his manner in class tends to arrogance', but by the time he was fourteen one of his masters would write: 'I feel I must comment on the very real help Sebastian gives to Danny.' By one of those strange twists of coincidence, the future Olympic champion had become friendly with Danny Heffernan, a boy afflicted with a burden of physical misfortune beyond the imagination of any normally fit person. Suffering when young from a rare form of juvenile arthritis, Danny received treatment which is at this time still a matter of arduous litigation. Whether or not the drugs treatment was responsible, Danny lost all but the quarter sight of one eye and his growth was retarded to the extent that, although the same age as Seb, he still has the build of an eleven-year-old. He has had countless operations, including both hips, yet in spite of all this, in spite of coordinating his own legal battle when able to read only Braille – though legal charities ultimately stepped in – he has retained one of the warmest and happiest dispositions you could meet, thanks in no small part to the friendship of Seb and his family. There were times, during periods of intense pain, when he was nursed as if one of the family by Angela and Peter.

❛ Danny and I had some rare old times at school. We had a nice little line going in orange drinks on sports day, only a penny or two, until we were rumbled, and there were other extramural trading deals in government surplus compasses and remaindered annuals! Danny was a marvellous character, he was so independent in spite of his handicap. It used to take a lot of self-control on my part when we were walking down the hill after school. He would insist on carrying his own briefcase and all the other boys would be belting past us while we had to go along at Danny's very slow pace. The way he has fought against his disability, living alone in his own purpose-built flat, and the way he has retained his sense of humour, are a lesson for us all. ❜

Seb's prowess was now such that one indulgent master would occasionally allow him to slip away from religious instruction periods to put in some extra training. In the winter of 1970-1, never out of the first three, he won the Yorkshire Schools cross-country title, and was building up towards the English Schools meeting at Luton. A week or so beforehand, Peter sent him out one afternoon for an easy distance run on the steep gradients of the surrounding streets. He got slightly carried away.

❛ Maybe it was my coming first in the Yorkshire,

maybe it was just natural enthusiasm, but I started racing a bus up one of the longer hills, ignoring Peter's instructions to take it easy. He was away on business and not there to pace me in the car as usual. I kept catching the bus up between stops and really having a bit of fun. It was sheer bravado. I came back home and said to Peter at supper time, 'you should have seen the bus driver's face!' Peter gradually became more and more angry, and I was so stiff I couldn't train for two days. I never again disregarded his training instructions and readily agreed, 'you make the decisions, I'll do the running', In recognition, I suppose, of my prospects at Luton, the school sent down two bus-loads of supporters. I ran like a drain and came twenty-fourth. I felt awful, but the other boys had had a nice day out, and I was allowed off homework for a couple of nights. 〕

Whatever that failure, any idea of becoming a professional footballer, thoughts of a trial with Sheffield Wednesday, were now in the past, and as for rugby, there was not much prospect for a half-pint of six and a half stone. His course was irrevocably settled, even though that summer, for the first and only time in his life, he came last in a 1,500 metres in the English Schools Championships.

〔 I'd had a mouth operation for some teeth trouble and had been out of action for five weeks, missing all my exams. I'd been staying down in Sidcup overnight before the race with friends who had a flat over a greengrocer's shop, with the result that I was awake at five in the morning. It was this experience, among others, which led Peter to devise a pre-race formula which I have been working to ever since, wherever circumstances permit. As Peter said, it was vital to produce myself friction-free for the race, physically and mentally fresh. The worst thing about schoolboys, and even some adults, is that they tend to run the race ten times beforehand and that's why it's so much better to keep out of the way. It does of course mean it's vital to know the race schedule and to be sure that it won't be altered. I was not popular with schoolmasters when Peter started insisting I should travel on the day of the race and not with the team, but there is no doubt about the psychological value of being away from a group. It led to some snide jokes around the northern circuit, that I would only arrive half an hour before the start in a plain black van, but I didn't mind that. By now I knew where I wanted to go, and I could put up with the difficulties which arose from being 'different'. On the occasion Angela remembers my saying that if I couldn't be successful at Athletics I would find a sport where I could be, there were quite a few friends present in the house – Ian Hague, for instance, a good 400 metres man who represents the essence of the sport, a purist who, while being my friend, has always been emphatic about what a great athlete Steve Ovett is, and others involved in the sport like Robert Hague and John Henson. My statement didn't offend them: there was just a stunned silence and it was clear to me I was simply operating on a different concept. George Gandy, who became my coach at Loughborough, has always said that quite apart from the physiological aspects required to be a champion there has to be an insatiable *need* to succeed. This has, if anything, grown over the years rather than diminished. **)**

The next two years saw a steady improvement in Seb's progress with the inevitable fluctuations which occur among boys growing at different rates in their teens. In 1972 he came tenth in the English Schools intermediate cross-country over four miles at Hillingdon, running against boys a year older – including Ovett who, at that time a 400 metres runner on the track, finished second. The following year, now sixteen, was a good one for him: he won the Yorkshire Schools 3,000 metres in very bad conditions at York in 8:49, then the English Schools 3,000 metres at Bebington in 8:40·2. To these victories were added the Northern Counties 1,500 metres in 3:59·5 – his first in under four minutes – and the Amateur Athletics Association Youth Championships 1,500 metres in 3:55. It was this result at Aldersley on 4 August, 1973, which more than any so far convinced Peter that Seb could go all the way.

(The next year was miserable. In the spring of 1974 I went on a national coaching week at Lilleshall, instead of a geography field week in Swanage, as a result of which I was decidedly unpopular with masters at Abbeydale Grange School, where I had moved after taking 'O' levels at Tapton. I was even less popular when, asked in class what Bakersfield, California was famous for – the largest refinery in the world – I replied instead, 'it's where Jim Ryun broke the world record for one mile in 1967 with 3:51·1. It wasn't long after that I found that I had two stress fractures and was unable even to train from the end of April to September. But I had a good winter, and early next year at Cleckheaton went under 3:50 for 1,500 metres for the first time with 3:49·7. Soon after this I had a minor injury, and as we never took risks, I went two weeks with no training. I hadn't really thought about the Yorkshire Senior Championships at the end of May, but after a few satisfactory 800 metres workouts Peter suddenly announced, in that dramatic way he rather fancies, 'we're going to run'. Aged eighteen, I was nervous and anxious about my first senior race. We went out to a jazz club that night and I stayed until after eleven, thinking to myself, 'has he flipped, or have I?' The following day I won, slowing up, against Walter Wilkinson, a hard, gritty Yorkshire train driver. If the British Athletics Board offered a Mercedes as an incentive, Walter would still get into the Olympic team today. He really was a competitor.

A personal best of 8:14·2 for 3,000 metres in the Northern Counties Under Twenty Championships at Blackburn ranked me junior number two in Europe, and I followed this with a personal best 3:47·1 to win the AAA Junior 1,500 metres. Now came my first experience of the strange lack of official cooperation which existed for so long at international level. I won the AAA with bad blisters, and asked if I could be excused the Junior International against France and Spain so as to get fit for the European Junior Championships in Athens. But I was obliged to run in the International.

Athens was a great experience for me. Dear Jim Coote, Athletics Correspondent of the *Daily Telegraph,* who was so committed and was always there even at many of the lesser meetings, had criticized my selection for Athens, saying I was selected on my record rather than my potential. I took no offence because he so obviously cared a lot about the sport, and it was a tragedy for all of us when he crashed piloting his own light aircraft down to Turin in 1979 for the Europa Cup Final. I loved the heat in Athens and I was really relaxed before the race – so relaxed that I fell asleep on a couch in an empty dressing-room under the stadium an hour before the final, and only woke up eighteen minutes before the start. Although I ran a new personal best of 3:45·2, I was third behind Ari Paunonen of Finland. I remember afterwards receiving a lecture from Mrs Nelson Neale, a nice old lady who, I was told, was a Women's AAA coach even though she seemed well into her seventies. She told me very earnestly how Sydney Wooderson's failing in pre-war days had been that he couldn't change pace and that this was why I had lost. I thanked her, but I couldn't help smiling.

The one thing that really did irritate me, an indication of the kind of immaturity and irresponsibility which often exists in British teams travelling abroad, was that while I was asleep one night in the student village somebody took all my racing kit, and pinned a ransom note on the wall saying it would turn up again 'in Moscow 1980'! I don't think it affected my equilibrium, it just seemed silly. On the way back, coming through customs at London, people put a lot of excess duty-free stuff on my trolley, voting me the one with the most innocent face. I was the only one who got stopped! **)**

2: Life with Father

❛ The partnership with my father has worked because I like the guy. I would like him even if he were not my father. He can be a bit brutal, certainly, but he has been right so often. When I was only thirteen he drew up a projection of progress for me to 1980 with an optimum 1,500 metres time of 3:30, and that at a time when I had achieved only 4:31·8 and the world record was still Jim Ryun's 3:33·1 in Los Angeles in 1967. So often over the years he's had more faith in me than I have had in myself. I know I can rely on him one hundred per cent. Anyone who levels the accusation that he was on an ego trip, that he was force-feeding me, is way off the mark. I never complained because I shared with him the hope and ambition that he always had for me. There's no county in England to rival Yorkshire for the mile talent which has come out of it, with men like Ibbotson and Simpson, but initially a lot of people thought my old man was right off his head. 'He's killing him', they would say, and Peter's reply would merely be, 'that's right, all the way to the top'. His greatest achievement, I think, was in getting me over the difficult transitional period from junior to senior ranks four or five years ago. When I was seventeen he said to me that if ever I felt I was not going far enough or fast enough with him, that I needed a different coach, I should say so. But the moment passed, and I never doubted him.

There was no recrimination from either side over poor results. We were both free agents. If anything ever struck me as crazy, I'd say so beforehand. Even after Prague in 1978, when we agreed I should run from the front and got well beaten into third place, there were no problems. Some critics thought we were both mad, but it was no lie when Peter said, 'I learnt more from that one race than anything in the whole year'. What is special about him as a coach is that he thinks on his feet, as they say in the north. He is one of nature's survivors. There's nothing I do that isn't thought out, not a single action is casual. But he's not a motivator

31

– that's not necessary in either training or racing because I'm a self-motivator. Funnily enough, one of the most important features of our relationship, possibly the key, is that he knew nothing about coaching when he started! The fact that he didn't compete left him without mental barriers on what is physically possible.

If he'd competed, even at a lesser level, he would have had an idea what 10 × 400 metres in 60 seconds actually *feels* like, and he would have been conditioned by that. On the physiological side he's read very widely. His talent is as much in *management* as in coaching. In the early days he would go out and find the right advice on technicalities. Now he doesn't need much advice. There was a time when he was continually going to coaching and physiology conferences, constantly picking people's brains. That is where George Gandy has been so valuable to us, with his specialist knowledge in bio-mechanics. ❵

George Gandy, a tall, dark, sardonic humourist, athletics consultant to Sudan and the Irish Army, is a man whose rolling glances, from behind heavy rimmed glasses, occasionally give him the air of a Balkan spy in a Bond thriller. Such an air befits someone who possesses a Greek-like capacity for getting his own way without anyone noticing. He is not only an authority on bio-mechanics, but is an athletics coach of considerable perception who has been responsible for much of Loughborough University's prominence in recent years. His contribution to Seb's progress, the humour apart, has been a vital one with winter speed work, circuit training, and weight training, in the thirty weeks of the academic year when Seb has unavoidably been separated from Peter.

In the winter prior to his three world records in 1979, Seb, still maintaining a full academic life at Loughborough, trained no more than fifty miles a week, which by international standards of the day was strangely low when the school of thought since 1960 was that mileage made champions. Led by the coaching example of New Zealander Arthur Lydiard, who trained Peter Snell and others, at least one hundred miles a week had become the norm, and indeed there were those who trained far in excess of this, with the result that many of them ultimately and inevitably broke down with muscle and joint injuries. It was Peter

32

Coe who reminded everyone that quantity was no substitute for quality.

     6 Round about the end of my junior career we really decided there had to be a change of emphasis. I was being labelled a 1,500 metres or 3,000 metres runner at eighteen. By twenty-one I'd probably have been running 5,000 metres; before I was thirty I would have been running marathons. That was not what I wanted. I wanted to run 1,500 metres. There's only a limited possibility of improvement in distance work, going up and up and up, but coming back down again we could see the benefits were very much better. I needed the leg speed. My stride length had never been a problem, but on occasion maintaining a fast cadence was. I wasn't going to be able to develop my cadence or my sprinting abilities just from running distances or going up the clock all the time. I had to be getting in with the sprinters, I had to find out what it was actually like to sprint. That was really the side of my Loughborough career, when I started training with George in the winter months, developing leg speed with weight training and speed drills. My advice, if anybody wants it, is not to get too far away from the basis of what you are doing, because modern 800 metres and 1,500 metres running demands a considerable amount of leg speed and you're not going to get it from running slowly in training. You have to develop and train the mind, as well as the body, to run fast. A lot of it is coordination. You cannot improve your basic speed, unfortunately. It's a fact that we are born with what we are born with. You can't alter your muscle composition. The important thing is to work on strengths and not on weaknesses. Sometimes in the winter of 1978 and 1979 my mileage was considerably less than fifty a week. Obviously I don't need so many miles because of my light build, and I am not willing to smash my feet and knees out on the road. I am lucky that I've never needed to cram in the distance work' 9

Was not the double relationship with Peter, as athlete and son, inhibiting?

     6 No, it's the proof of the success of our coach/athlete relationship that I didn't feel the need to escape from him in the

33

home, that we could coexist happily acros the dinner table. But I have never allowed him to organize my life outside athletics. His attitude on matters away from athletics is, 'that's my advice on my experience, it's up to you what you do with it'. From his own family, he has brought a great unity to us as a family and we always show a united public front. He's been criticized for talking about 'my athlete', rather than 'my son', or telling people *'we're* going to run in Oslo'. But I would say in just the same way *'we're* going to run a 1,500', it's something we're in together. Certainly, he's a hard man. I know from the men down at the cutlery factory where's he's production director, and where I've worked in the holidays. They've told me: 'He's tough but fair. He's consistent, you always know where you stand with him.'

Once, when we were having dinner, there was a call from the works manager. 'The bloody factory's on fire' Peter said, as he dashed out of the front door and down the hill in the car through all the red lights. It was all a bit of a farce, the fire-brigade couldn't find it and rang up in the middle of the fire to ask for the post code! The block was shared with another business which the company had attempted to buy out several times. It was this, in fact, which was now on fire, and not Peter's own factory. 'It looks like it's yours overnight', said the dejected owner as he stood beside Peter, surveying the smoking, gutted building. 'I was going to pull it down anyway', Peter said rather crushingly!

People who infer, from his public reaction to the mess I made of the 800 metres in Moscow, that he dominates me would not have thought the same had they been there at the open-air café in the Olympic Village when I learned what he had said to the press the day after the race. I told him quite emphatically, 'you're supposed to be an articulate man, but your choice of words was naïve. I'll accept the criticism from you direct, but I won't take it from you via the press.' Peter can be too trusting in assuming the best in people who have power like the press. You can be friendly with the media on a personal basis, but in the final analysis they have a job to do, and that will always be their priority ahead of personal allegiance. So you have to be guarded in moments of stress, in the same way that, say, you wouldn't let foreigners see round certain areas of your factory. If Peter was humiliated and ashamed by my bumbling performance in the 800 metres, he had reason to be, but he should have been more discreet. What he said was the sort of direct thing that comes naturally to him, and I

34

wouldn't try to change a man of sixty. But people just didn't understand. When a coach has given twelve years driving towards a peak, and an athlete of my standing then runs so ineptly, the coach *is* going to feel slightly humiliated. But his reaction in public added to the illusion that I do only what I am told, that he puts the boot in, that he has no feeling for me, and that it was he who had been hurt. People can only equate our relationship with their own with their fathers. Maybe some of the people who were heavy on Peter had a distant or unsatisfactory relationship with their fathers. He brought the trouble on himself after the 800 metres by his open frankness, his choice of adjectives, but as he said to me after the severe press reaction, 'I suppose they just don't understand'. If I'd failed again in the 1,500 metres, we'd both have got a lot more stick. Other coaches spend as much time or more with their athletes, but they don't get the same criticism if the athlete loses. It was crazy, for instance, that the consensus of opinion after Prague was that Peter had lost me the race. **)**

Climbing up out of Sheffield on the A57 towards Glossop and Manchester, past the neat semis and bungalows with their tidy front gardens in the only conservative constituency in South Yorkshire, the road winds down again before rising past the Howden reservoirs to Hollow Meadows. Cocooned in the driver's car, the harsh April wind outside, which rips across the barren moors, seems no inconvenience. Eventually we come to a turning on the right. It is the start of a ten mile run across some of the most exposed country in England. A farmer in gaiters is busily unconcerned in his barn, with its leaning, undulating roof. As we pull up in the loose stones on the edge of the unfenced road, a sheep dog bounds across and barks at us because there is nothing better to do. The runner gets out of the front passenger seat in his track-suit, and the east wind grabs at the open door. The driver checks the stop watch round his neck and the runner sets off across the moonscape. It takes him the first mile to pick up his rhythm, to begin to get really warm, and as we climb, the speedometer hovering around 10 m.p.h. in second gear, the view of the reservoirs opens up far below. The heather and last year's matted, crumbling bracken are now almost head high on the steep banks as the runner starts to push harder and the driver has to accelerate to keep pace. There is not a soul in sight, just the

35

occasional morose looking ewe nibbling away at dead pasture as appetizing as a scrubbing brush. The driver glances at the watch and gives a nod of approval. The real destination is still a long way off; but it is up here, far from the the omnivorous eye of television, that the critical work is done. The driver says, 'the danger is of being complacent, to let it become easy, but at the back of your mind you know that other lonely men around the world are grinding it out just like this'.

Following a few yards behind, one becomes mesmerized by the clockwork motion of the slim figure pounding away over the tarmac, leaning into the head wind. A thin sun comes through the cloud, and you hope that some of the warmth is reflected onto the runner off the high stone wall which now skirts the road. 'He always drives hard into the inclines, then takes it easy down hill', says the man at the wheel, hunching forward as if to try to help the runner. 'It's so tempting to do it the other way round, to go easy up the hills, then open out when the gradient flattens.' The road now runs through a little sheltered niche between the hills, with ivy and bramble tumbling over the high walls. The route twists and turns downwards again towards the village of Low Bradfield, and now the runner is really flowing at well under six minutes to the mile.

We glide through the village, past the pub and the post office, and the green with its cricket square in roped-off cold storage. A woman with a shopping basket turns to her companion with a nudge which says, 'it's him'. We turn round the end of the reservoir, alongside the pines which fringe the water. A couple of crews, also out training, rest gratefully on their sixteen oars, their eyes devouring in unison the figure flitting so swiftly past the trees, oblivious momentarily of their own objectives as they study someone whose destiny has in past months been the discussion of almost every sportsman in the land. The road climbs again, up past smarter houses now, and the next mile slips by in a little over five minutes. Eventually we pull up outside a pub, the ten mile mark, not an oasis of respite. The runner walks back to the car breathing hard but not in discomfort, and rests his head on his arms on the car roof. The driver winds down the window and puts a fond hand on the pale blue track-suit to measure and record the heart-beat. They exchange a smile and the runner says simply, 'that was good'. He has done it a hundred times before, but each time the experience is different. Today the wind made it particu-

36

larly hard, but both the runner and the driver know that things are going well.

⁣ I've trained over the peaks from the age of eleven or twelve. Often I was running with senior athletes and I have always enjoyed it, the loneliness, the solitude up among the pine forests on a Sunday morning. I find the remoteness up there so stimulating, especially when there is a white-out and there are no other cars about. Some days, when Sheffield and Manchester are cut off from each other by snow, there's a sense of total isolation only a few miles from the house. The weather in the winter is so uncertain, it can be really cutting when the fog and ice close in. I've been out on occasions wearing three tracksuits and a waterproof. On some runs I've come back with my eyelashes frozen. The day before Christmas last winter it was really miserable when I did fourteen or fifteen miles and I came back drenched through. In a running family, that's business as usual. But whatever the weather, it's always exhilarating in a funny sort of way, the challenge of beating the elements.

I would do it even if I was not aiming for the Olympics or world records. It's something which most of my friends who have quit racing do regularly on a Sunday. It's difficult to describe why, unless you've been up there and come round the shoulder of a hill, and there suddenly is the whole of Sheffield laid out miles below. I've never felt frustrated up there the way I have working on the track, because up there you are surrounded by beauty. I always think it is silly the way the north of England is so badly promoted by the situation comedies on television, the image of Coronation Street and satanic mills, when we have so much beauty so close to the people in the northern cities. ⁣

Almost the only flat stretch of road around Sheffield runs through the Rivelin Valley, between precipitous farm land on one side and wooded hills and allotments on the other. Alongside the road, hidden among trees, is a stream and a protected nature walk. It is along this road, a fraction over three miles before it hits the city near the Sheffield Wednesday football ground, that some of the most remarkable runs of all time have been made, observed only by mothers with prams and a few disinterested motorists.

Along this stretch it is possible to fit in six consecutive half-miles, and it is these sequences that have built in Seb the exceptional stamina which, until a couple of years ago, none but Peter knew he possessed. So impressive were the figures, so revealing of the young student's potential, that he and his coach resisted all requests to come and film him in action. It is here that the positions of runner and driver are reversed, with Peter moving ahead to pace his athlete, and draw him out occasionally to some quite exceptional times. On one of the days when I was there he did a sequence of six, with recovery intervals of only a minute and a half between each, and the third of the series was almost fast enough to qualify for the semi-final of the 800 metres in one of the six first-round heats in Moscow. 'He's feeling rather pleased with himself, and he's entitled to', observed Peter, as we pulled up at the finish of the series near a bus stop of afternoon giggling schoolgirls. They didn't recognize the slim young man standing there on the pavement with heaving chest. Just another of those funny joggers they thought, no doubt, as they stared a trifle embarrassed. Within two minutes of the finish of this gruelling session Seb's pulse rate was back down to only 86, and off he went on a two-mile warm-down. The ring-master was pleased. He'd gently needled the performer before the start about whether he was in shape. That was no breach of their trust. Peter said:

'I've never ever told him a false time to encourage him. Whoever beats him is going to know he has been in a race. I may not be the best coach in the world, but what I am doing for Seb is right – which is not to say someone else might not do it better. It's true that I came to it fresh, that I wasn't conditioned by training dogmas handed down through the generations. Because I was so involved with him, people thought we must be doing a hundred miles a week, when in fact we were doing under thirty when he came third in Athens in the European Junior. There is nothing basically wrong with a parent being a coach, though I have seen many kids damaged by their fathers trying to overcome their own deficiences through the child's achievements. What has helped, though it may sound élitist, is an intelligent approach to the problems. Mechanical engineering has actually been a help, too, in bringing him through his adolescence. Running, in my opinion, is to a great extent science-based, but it is also an art, because science does not offer all the answers. Managing an engineering business successfully demands co-ordination in a whole range of aspects. To get something done, you call upon the best resources. When I came into athletics I didn't know much about physiology, but I knew of people who did. There was any amount of advice, but so much of it conflicting. So I did a lot of reading and went to conferences and listened to a lot of people – and discarded much of what I read and heard. I discovered what Astrand, the Swedish sports physiologist, and the German Gerschler had written. But I realized that nobody actually *knew* for sure. There is nothing revolutionary in what I have done with Seb, but it has been tailor-made for his physique. An athlete to a great extent determines his own training by his responses to the tasks you set for him and by his racing results. The coach must adjust to the athlete.

'Seb is not a mindless automaton who would go out and run unquestioningly, but I have had to be certain that he would adhere to the programme when I was not there, yet that he would vary it when necessary because of the weather. He is exceptional because his trust in me is total. The coach can only work with the athlete's consent. The measure of the athlete is the extent of his consenting to do things within his capacity. But the danger for the coach is that if the athlete's trust is total, he may consent to anything.

'In conversation with other coaches, I've not heard of one athlete who is as dedicated as Seb though, admittedly, I don't know all the athletes abroad, and one knows that some in the past such as Elliott trained phenomenally hard. I'm far from perfect and, although Seb says he gets on well with me, I think his going to Loughborough was important. The strain of eating and sleeping under the same roof over the last four years, at the same time as the racing pressure on him increased, too, might have become too much. Yet we have only had one serious disagreement and that was before his first world records, but it had nothing to do with athletics. Events really began to change with the sudden acceleration of Seb's progress in the summer of 1979, though how much this was a result of relief at getting his degree it would be hard to say. Certainly it came a year earlier than I had reckoned. I expected him to get down *near* Juantorena's 800 metres world record of 1:43·4, maybe clip a bit off by September, but not take a whole second off in July! Possibly what pleased me most was that he did it on his own, and I sensed a qualitative change in his make-up. My real joy was not only the record, but that it was one in the eye for all those who suggested he couldn't do anything without his Dad. I can't break any records, but what I can say is that I have managed to produce a runner in the round.

'Of course his first three world records were a triumph and of course I had some reflected glory, but coaching someone from youth is all about weaning. The athlete should be coach-orientated, but should not become coach-dependent. My success was that he went out to Oslo for the 800 metres, assessed the situation, picked up the 'phone and said, "this is what I think". He had gone there with instructions to win a tactical race. I said, "if what you tell me is correct, then go for the time instead of the win". You teach an athlete to train as much as to race. When he went to the front 450 metres from the finish of the Oslo Golden Mile it was the sign of an intelligent runner. He was in unknown territory, and he'd only run a handful of four-lap races, but his instinct told him to capitalize on his strength at that moment. I'd told him the tactics would probably be dictated to him, but he suddenly knew he had to make the decisions.'

❝ I suppose you could say my father could now die a happy man. He's seen the satisfactory culmination of fifteen years' work, and certainly he'll retire the day I quit. He's done what he set out to do, and from now on it can no longer be the same. We talked about it quite a bit before the Olympics, knowing that his role would change quite considerably from then on. I sensed for him, that while there was still a lot to go for – world records and medals – they could never produce the same feeling for him as the first time. He's quite sentimental at heart, more than you'd suppose. A year ago or so Kenny Moore, the American marathon runner, and writer for *Sports Illustrated*, was staying with us, and talked about giving us a dog. Peter was quite put out. 'There's no way he's going to pull that one on us, we'll have no bloody animal in this house.' On Christmas Eve, Kenny turned up on the doorstep with a small round puppy wagging its tail, and Peter just looked at it and said, 'Oh, well. What are we going to call it?' ❞

3: Rivalry

The 1977 edition of *Athletics* – that excellent annual fund of information and statistics edited by Ron Pickering and Mel Watman, now regrettably discontinued – contained no entry for Sebastian Coe under its section 'Who's Who in the British team', for the good reason that he was not in the team the previous season when only nineteen. Steve Ovett, on the other hand, born a year earlier than Coe in 1955 in Brighton, merited an entry of eleven lines. He had won the 1973 European Junior 800 metres and a silver medal a year later, aged nineteen, among the seniors in Rome. In 1975 he won the Europa Cup 800 metres, was a disappointed fifth off the outside lane in the Montreal Olympics, and was unquestionably the golden boy of British middle distance running. With a build almost four inches taller than Coe, at 6 feet 1 inch, and 25 pounds heavier at 11 stone, he was, for traditionalists, the 'good big 'un' who would always beat the 'good little 'un'. The emergence of a young student from Loughborough, whose academic schedule postponed the start of his serious racing season until the middle of each summer, posed little threat to the sumptuously equipped former art student from Brighton. Or did it?

    ❝ I first realized that from Steve's point of view I was more than just another rival at the end of the 1977 season, which was my first major outdoor season. Little comments had come my way. For instance, when asked what he thought of my prospects, he thought I would 'never be fast enough to run a really world class 800 metres'. It was only a few weeks after that remark that I broke Andy Carter's U.K. record, running second behind Mike Boit in the Coca-Cola at Crystal Palace, and being the first Briton under 1:45, with 1:44·95. I always had the feeling that when the gap began to disappear – Steve's best up to then was 1:45·4 – the rivalry would become geater, and with it his need to prove himself. To an extent, of course, it did us both good. Sport thrives on rivalry and colour. Bayi v Walker had been a huge talking point leading up to the Montreal Olympics and then, sadly, never occurred because of the African boycott. But, as with Ryun v Keino, Pirie v Kuts, or Bannister v Landy, they were not from the same country. The *real* intensity occurs when you get two men from the same country, such as Hägg and Andersson, who broke each other's 1,500 metres and mile records eight times between 1941 and 1945. What has made it so interesting in the case of Steve and me, I feel, is that we are both so different, not just physically but in attitudes, too. After my record in the Coke I was surprised when Steve, who was the fellow with the reputation, ignored me in the warm-up area. Dave Jenkins said to me, 'he's like that'. I wondered why. **)**

The previous season, 1976, in which Seb and his coach had decided that they must move away from the 5,000 metres and concentrate on basic speed, Seb was running experimentally in the main. In the Kraft Games, bidding for Olympic selection, in his own opinion he had run badly in the 1,500 metres, in spite of a personal best of 3:43·2, finishing seventh. There had been another hassle with the authorities because he was in the middle of exams and had trouble getting to Crystal Palace on time. In the AAA final, after only three weeks' serious training, he improved his time marginally with 3:42·6, to finish fourth behind Dixon, Moorcroft, and Clement, beating off a challenge from Quax. The next week at Gateshead, running in gale conditions and setting the pace from the front, he finished third in the mile behind Walker and Moorcroft. Back at Crystal Palace, still experimenting, he led for three laps in the Emsley Carr Mile, was brushed aside on the final bend by Malinowski's elbow, and faded on the run in to finish seventh, in spite of beating four minutes for the first time with 3:58·3. Moorcroft won a fine race from Bayi.

(I particularly wanted to get under four minutes, so I had to run from the front to extend myself. I had nothing to learn from hanging back among the pack. Peter and I had always believed, even when I was younger, that it was important to go out and *commit* yourself, it is the only way to find out about

42

yourself and others. If I'd sat with the pack I would have been out-kicked even earlier, finishing outside four minutes, and learning nothing . . . except that I hadn't got a kick, as yet. I was encouraged a lot by these races and it was now, during the winter at Loughborough, that I began to gain the benefit of the speed and weight training with George. He made me a lot stronger. I ventured into my first indoor track 'season', ran a 600 metres before Christmas in 1:19·7, and won the U.K. Indoor 800 metres in 1:49·1, my first senior title. I was really beginning to feel in control of my strength and my legs, and followed it up with the 800 metres U.K. record against Germany in Dortmund, and a Commonwealth indoor record of 1:47·5, against France at Cosford, leading all the way. **)**

It was a small British team spearheaded by Seb which went to the European Indoor Championships in San Sebastian in 1977. We flew to Bilbao, and thence took a mini-bus to San Sebastian's picturesque bay. Seb and I chatted on the way out, and shortly afterwards he was surprised when he was given a stern warning by the formidable Marea Hartman that he would be well advised, for reasons about which she was not specific, to steer well clear of both me and Ron Pickering. Some of those with administrative power in amateur sport and who, in their honorary positions, in many instances enjoy a status which far exceeds that of their daily working or social life, do not take kindly to the enquiring eye and ear of the media.

It was a memorable occasion for both Seb and young Jane Colebrook, coached by their father and mother respectively, each winning the 800 metres. Jane slaughtered the combined might of Eastern Europe to equal the world best of 2:1·1, while Seb, leading from gun to tape, was a tenth of a second outside the Italian Carlo Grippo's world record with 1:46·5.

(I was on cloud nine, and I felt I had every right to be. With no international experience until two weeks before, I had won a European title. Peter was delighted that I had done it on my own and had run from the front, but I must admit that the tactics were partly inspired by some lurid stories from the knowledgeable Cliff Temple of *The Sunday Times*, who had opened my eyes with his description of blood all over the boards from ripped tendons. I was also amused and surprised by my first experience of British management abroad. Our manager was the amiable, avuncular Bob Stinson, a former Achilles runner. He has done valuable work in formulating British proposals to the International Federation aimed at rationalizing the anomalies of so-called amateur athletics, and his legal mind is a valuable factor in trying to achieve a balance between progress and tradition. But he was an exceedingly low-key manager! While other coaches were rushing around shouting, Stinson simply looked at me rather balefully when the time came for me to leave the warm-up area and go out for the final, and his only comment was 'well, bye-bye then'. In fact, I quite like that kind of detachment, I don't want instructions or advice from any official other than my coach.

Ten days later I damaged an achilles tendon and was out of action for fourteen weeks; not running again until July in one of Geoff Capes's enjoyable Dewhurst meetings at Spalding. I came second in the AAA 800 metres behind Savic of Yugoslavia, running well above my level of fitness, to beat that big-hearted competitor Walker with 1:46·8. Against expectation, in view of my injury. I was selected for the Europa Cup Final in Helsinki. 〉

There was an outside hope that, if everything went well, Britain might have ousted one of the East European state 'machines', Russia or East Germany, for a place in the eight-nation World Cup, due to take place in Düsseldorf. In the event, both men's and women's teams performed satisfactorily to come fourth and third respectively. But the men's 800 metres was a farce. Running wide off the final bend and making ground fast on the leaders, Seb was disgracefully given a short-arm tackle by Willy Wulbeck as the West German suddenly switched lanes from the inside and went on to win in 1:47·21. After losing several strides, Seb finished fourth behind Beyer of East Germany and Marajo of France. Wulbeck should certainly have been disqualified for an outrageous foul, but the appeal jury rejected Britain's immediate protest after looking at the video recording. It was Seb's first bad international experience.

❝ I was reluctant at the time to say so, it sounded presumptuous, but I felt I had been going to win because I had just gone past Wulbeck and was gaining on the others. But I was a real novice, it was my first senior outdoor international and I was taken aback by such tactics. I felt awful about it afterwards, both shins had been spiked and the *Daily Telegraph* didn't help matters by saying that I 'appeared to stumble'. I ran the five miles back to the hall of residence thinking that if I had been fit enough I could have gone to the front earlier. It had no lasting significance, however, other than the lingering doubt at the back of my mind that I was vulnerable to the hand-off, and that winter I stepped up my weight training with George.

Two days later I was in Brussels for the Ivo Van Damme Memorial, and ran a personal best of 1:46·3 to take third place in the 800 metres behind Boit and Enyeart. Running against West Germany at Crystal Palace a week later I won the 800 metres and, as I was leaving the stadium, I was asked by Brian Hewson and Mike Farrell, the organizers, if I would run the Emsley Carr Mile the next day. One of the Sunday papers said it was a 'reward' from the British Board, but the fact was there was no one else. ❞

Out-kicking Bayi in the final straight for a sub-56 last quarter-mile, Seb recorded 3:57·7 to become the youngest winner of the event, though it is interesting to reflect that his time, run at the age of twenty, would be substantially improved by teenagers Graham Williamson and Steve Cram within the next three years. It was the first time that Seb had earned a back-page headline, with the *Mirror*'s 'Bold King Coe' on the Monday morning. Yet although Coe had now gained the U.K. record at 800 metres in the Coke, Ovett held both the 1,500 metres and the mile, with Seb not even ranked in the U.K. all-time top ten. His rise had passed largely unnoticed in academic circles at Loughborough, too. When a BBC film crew enquired if they could set up a unit to film a sequence of Sebastian Coe in the library, the librarian queried, 'do you mean the one who comes in here on Friday mornings to read *Athletics Weekly*?'

Early in 1978 he suffered a serious injury, putting his foot down an old gate-post hole while out training at Loughborough, was lucky not to break the ankle, and severely ruptured all the tendons. He sat in agony while his sock expanded like a balloon as he watched it. He crawled across the field to a security car that happened to be there on the campus and was rushed to hospital by George.

❦ I was carried pick-a-back 200 yards from the car park to Casualty, where it was the usual Sunday scene: kids who'd fallen off swings at the playground, etc. . . . I sat with my leg in a sling for an hour and eventually was taken to the X-ray department, where the Sister said it was broken. George insisted it wasn't. Sister: 'I'm telling you it is.' George: 'I'm not a betting man' (which was a bare-faced lie because he would bet on two earwigs climbing a wall), 'but I'll put my shirt on it that it's not.' Sister: 'What are your qualifications?' George: 'MSc in bio-mechanics.' Whereupon she immediately started calling him 'Dad'. The X-ray attendant cheerfully volunteered: 'It's so bad that if it's not broken, it would be better if it was!' The Sister now insisted it should be put in plaster. George: 'No, there'll be muscle wastage and we won't be able to give him physiotherapy.' Sister: 'Get out of here at once.' I was wheeled towards the plaster room. George: 'Do you realize you are dealing with the fastest 800 metre runner in the world?' Defiant Sister: 'Well, he'll just have to be the slowest for a change.'

I sat there listening to this row as if it was all happening to somebody else. George promptly discharged me, and the sequel was that when we saw a consultant the following morning, Peter having come down from Sheffield, the Sister threatened to report George to the Medical Council for impersonating my father – which of course he hadn't. The consultant insisted that it would take me six months to recover, but I went to see George Preston, a marvellous physiotherapist who used to be with Leicester City F.C., and within ten days I was jogging again, which tells you a lot about the quality of sports medicine in general practice in Britain.

Initially I was running in intense pain – the only time we have ever hurried an injury. I lost about a month of flat-out preparation, and then went on holiday with the family to the Adriatic, where it was really too hot for training and my weight went down a stone to only 8·5 – the result of trying to do too much too quickly. Peter worked brilliantly to get me back into some sort of shape for the selection trials for the European Championships.

We'd previously decided that I would not attempt the Commonwealth Games, that the real challenge would lie in Prague. I managed to win the selection race, the U.K. Championships at Meadowbank, after being disqualified initially for breaking lane too early at the end of the stagger. I hadn't. **)**

A fortnight before going to Prague for the European Championships, Seb was at his favourite Van Damme meeting in Brussels, lowering his own 800 metres U.K. record to 1:44·3 ahead of American James Robinson and Marajo of France. A first lap of 50·5 showed that he'd got back much of the lost ground and, remarkably, he was now getting within range of Juantorena's record of 1:43·4. Moreover, as he set off for Prague it was with the knowledge that he was now the fastest in Europe and over a second inside Ovett's best time to date, his 1:45·4 in 1976. But Seb soon ran into problems.

(Prague was cold, wet and wretched. The accommodation was gloomy, the food was poor and unappetizing, and many of the team went down with a stomach bug. I was one of them and, with my weight *already* down to eight stone, it further drained my strength. In addition, I was quickly to discover that some athletes were more equal than others as far as the British Board were concerned. Not only had I been obliged to run in the trials where others had been excused, in spite of the fact that I was ranked first in Europe, but I was further annoyed to find that Steve was being allowed to postpone his decision on whether he would run the 800 metres in addition to the 1,500 metres right up to the last minute. Within what was supposed to be a team this was clearly unfair on the guy who was number one on times, but needed help in his first championships. Steve was saying he'd decide three or four hours before his heat, and the Board allowed him to play a psychological game with another member of the team. It's nice, even necessary, to know what you've got to face so that you can plan, though it doesn't bother me the same now. Steve appeared to try it again over Moscow, saying well on into the summer that he had a moral dilemma over Afghanistan, and that he didn't know if he would run; but I was sure he would. I'm not saying it would have made any difference to the situation if I had known in Prague whether he was running or not, but it would have reduced the pressure on me. The Board have never taken a strong line with him. To make matters worse, Harry Wilson, who was national coach for middle distances and was out there in that capacity with the team, was also Steve's personal coach and spent much of the time out of the village with Steve in an official car which was supposed to be available to all. On the night before the 800 metres final, Wilson was overheard on the stairs in the village saying to another athlete, 'as far as I'm concerned, there's no way Coe can beat Steve tomorrow'. In Prague he was officially as much my coach as Steve's, although of course Peter was out there with me. **)**

Both runners cruised through their semi-finals, Coe in 1:47·6, Ovett in 1:46·5. Juantorena, there as a guest of his European 'brothers', said before the final: 'At this moment I think it will be Coe – but we ought to wait and see.' Reckoning that his chances depended on a scorching first leg which might drain Ovett, Seb went through the first lap in a blistering 49·3, the swiftest ever run. Down the back straight he held his lead, with Ovett tucked in behind and then the East German Olaf Beyer, a twenty-one-year-old maths student from Potsdam. As they came off the final bend Ovett pounced to overtake the now fading Seb – but he had been trailing the wrong man. Fifty yards from the tape Beyer edged past Ovett, and the British pair, who had been regarded as certainties throughout Europe for the first two places, had to settle for silver and bronze. Ovett's 1:44·1 lowered Coe's two-week-old record, and Beyer's 1:43·8 was the fifth fastest of all time and a tenth outside the Italian Fiasconaro's European record. There was no sign of Ovett's by now famous wave as he covered his face with his hands in dismay. He then refused to attend the official Czech press conference, saying he had no need of 'useless publicity'.

(The extraordinary thing about Beyer was that Steve and I didn't see him again for ages. As he ran through the finishing line he was wrapped in blankets by two officials and hurried from the arena, instead of going off on a lap of honour, as you would expect from someone who had just won a European title. Geoff Capes and Dave Jenkins say that he walked off with his eyes completely slack. And he then went missing. We were informed that he'd provided his urine sample within thirteen minutes of running 1:43, which is unusual to say the least. It took Steve and me almost an hour and a half, and we only saw Beyer again at the victory ceremony. **)**

Such is the widespread incidence of the use of stimulants, particularly in the United States and Eastern Europe, that suspicions inevitably arise when an athlete behaves as strangely as Beyer did in Prague, and nothing he has done since has upheld that performance.

(It had always been my intention to run from the front; Peter and I wanted to test the concept that no one can kick off sub-1:44 pace, or even sub-1:45. And it proved it. What happened was that I slowed the most, then Steve, with Beyer managing to sustain his speed that little bit longer. Approaching world record pace it comes down to who fades the least. Kicking is not a last 200 metres in 26, it's in 23. A 26 is just maintaining your form. In that race, the guy who did the least for most of the race was first and I did the most and was third. Brendan Foster had agreed with my plan, saying, 'right, even if you risk failing, do it that way'. Most people thought I was nuts, though Adrian Metcalfe was one of the few who had anything good to say: 'I take my hat off to anyone who has the guts to go out and run in a championship at that initial pace.' Steve said afterwards that he reckoned that if he'd made his effort at 200 metres instead of 90 he might have won, but I feel that at the pace of that race he would have simply faded earlier.

Both Peter and I thought that a sub-50 first lap would be possible at some future date when I was fit. People were inclined to forget that Prague was my first championship with heats and semi-finals, and there was the fact that my weight was seriously down and my ankle was swelling after every run. The thing about athletics is that it is like poker sometimes: you know what's in your hand, and it may be a load of old rubbish, but you have to keep up a front! I went to Prague hoping to make the most of the psychological advantage of my time in Brussels, but knowing that it was not really representative of what I was consistently capable of at that time. The lesson Prague really taught me was never again to reckon on only one opponent in the field. Somewhere at this very moment, training far away from the sophisticated media and without all the pressures, there's probably someone running at altitude in Kenya or Mexico who is suddenly going to appear out of the blue, and we will know very little about him. That is great – as it should be. **)**

Peter looks for the iron in a runner. 'I want to see what the bastards are made of' he said before the race. My opinion is that the result in Prague did more than anything, when the time came, to persuade Peter and Seb not to run from the front in Moscow – when the justification for doing so was in fact far greater. It is significant that Peter said to me after Prague not only that he had learned much about reactions to world record pace, but that front running would always be risky and that the man with the basic speed would always be safer running from the back. Peter:

'Seb had, and still has, the ability and the bravery to do whatever is necessary to learn and improve, whatever the cost at the time. He could have blamed Prague on me, but in spite of being miserable he did not then or subsequently ever reproach me. He was in there to apply maximum pressure on others and that's what he did. The result wasn't bad for a part-timer in the fifth fastest race ever. We had already decided that for 1979-80 he would become full-time, we knew that in 1978 he was nowhere near the limit of his training schedules.'

(After Prague I reckoned it would do me good to run a two miles in the Coca-Cola to end off the season. Brendan, who has been a very good friend and counsellor, had thought it was a good idea, too, but in Prague, before we left, Alan Pascoe came up to me and told me I was down for the 800 metres. I said I wanted the two miles but Andy Norman, the Southern Counties AAA official who has done an enormous amount to help promote sponsored international meetings in Britain and is now an international selector, told me that the 800 metres was going to be very good, with both Wulbeck and Boit in the field. But they both pulled out before the day, and Norman subsequently told Brendan that I had been kept out of the two miles because Steve didn't want me in the race. I felt flattered. The 800 metres ended up being a totally domestic affair, and I managed to get back the U.K. record from Steve, being the first Briton under 1:44 with 1:43·95 ahead of Dane Joseph. Again Steve ignored me after the record that night, and Peter couldn't resist quipping to Harry Wilson before we left the stadium: 'Congratulate Steve on his two mile record, but just tell him we always considered the 800 metres record was only borrowed!'

The same night Steve had set a world two mile best of 8:13·5, beating Brendan's record, and in the process he defeated the sensational Henry Rono, who that year had established a unique quartet of world records at 3,000 metres, 5,000 metres, 10,000 metres, and the 3,000 metres steeplechase. But Steve treated him shoddily when he was tired, coming level with him in the finishing straight, giving him a stare, and then waving as if to say goodbye as he sprinted for the tape. I really cannot condone so much of Steve's behaviour on and off the track. He is without question a wonderful athlete and my admiration of him as such is sincere and unbounded, but he does conduct himself in a way which has often left so much to be desired. He should not belittle inferior opponents in lesser races the way he sometimes has. That is sheer bad manners. **)**

Ovett's progress, the Prague 800 metres disappointment apart, had continued to be spectacular over four laps. Winning the Europa Cup 1,500 metres in Helsinki in 1977, then the World Cup in Düsseldorf with a U.K. record of 3:34·5 ahead of Wessinghage (West Germany) and Straub (GDR), with Walker sadly failing to finish, in Prague he had imperiously won the 1,500 metres in a championship record of 3:35·6 ahead of Coghlan (Eire) and Commonwealth champion Moorcroft.

(Many athletes can't help feeling that Steve has had kid-glove treatment from the Board. When he left the British team in the middle of a two-day match with West Germany in Bremen to go and run in Nijmegen in Holland, he received only a mild reprimand, whereas Jenkins in similar circumstances,

51

running abroad without formal clearance, was suspended from international competition. On the second day, why shouldn't Steve support those in the team who had supported him on the first? I can begin to understand his attitude towards the press, it's his business whether he talks to them or not, but I can't understand his attitude to other athletes. How could he claim before the Golden Mile in Oslo in 1979 that the race would be 'hollow' without him, that he had no need to pursue the other top milers around the world when he had nothing to prove? I still somehow expected him to turn up, but I was already beginning not to care. If he did, he did. It was the same in the Golden Mile in 1981. I'd had a conversation with his father at Crystal Palace before going to Oslo in 1979, he'd been very pleasant to me out in Prague. I asked him whether Steve was running in Oslo or not, and he replied, 'from what I understand he isn't'. Poor fellow, I thought to myself, you know as much as I do. After I broke the mile record in Oslo, Steve said, when asked whether he would congratulate me, 'why should I, it's not my record. I don't get caught up in times. I never run against the clock. I run against men on the day.' The evidence of the past three seasons, with endless record attempts, would seem to contradict this. **)**

Ovett had expressly stated that he would make 1979 a quiet year, prior to the Olympics, but John Rodda, the respected writer of the *Guardian*, felt obliged to say after the Golden Mile that 'Ovett must really eat those words about the victory in the race he missed being hollow'.

(I'd taken Steve's words at face value. What he said about a quiet year made sense after two or three hard seasons, why should he extend himself in the pre-Olympic year? For myself, I thought the international competition would do me good, though from the outset I made it clear I was willing to run for Britain in the Europa Cup semi-final and final, but did not wish to be selected for the World Cup in Montreal.

Steve had said so often, in *Athletics Weekly* and elsewhere, that world records didn't interest him, that all he cared about was winning races. When I set the world records in 1979 he said dismissively that if that was what gave me pleasure, it was up to me. Yet by August he had a carefully orchestrated record-breaking circus on the road with the help of Andy Norman. It seemed that my records forced him to break cover. He'd never previously exposed himself, running tactical races from the back to win in around 3:35/3:37. Steve's attitude to record breaking in 1979-81 has taken much of the romance and the unexpected element out of the sport. His two runs in Brussels in 1979 and 1980 were like moon-shots, Steve, the rocket, shedding pace-makers like bits of equipment all the way, until only the 'lunar module' was left to attempt the final 'landing'. I have never transported a clique of pace-makers with me when attempting records, and I have only ever made six deliberate record attempts – the 1,500 metres in Zürich in 1979 and 1980, and Stockholm in 1981, the 1,000 metres in Oslo in 1980 and 1981, and the mile in Zürich in 1981 – and in none of them did I know for sure who was going to be making the pace. When I set the record in 1979 in Zürich I had to run the last two laps on my own, and for the 800 metres and mile records in Oslo, Florence and Brussels there was no pacing specifically planned for me. **❯**

There is no doubt that at various times over recent years Ovett has exerted an influence on the composition of the field for races in which he would run. One of the most bizarre was in 1977 at Crystal Palace, when Juantorena would not run against Ovett, and Ovett would not run against Boit, so that Boit finished up running an almost meaningless 800 metres B race without serious opposition. Steve Scott, the American who finished second to Coe in the 1979 Golden Mile, insists that Ovett twice avoided him in early season races in 1980 in the States: 'Any conversation with Steve about athletics is shallow, because I can never be sure of what he is saying.' The BBC were left in no doubt, however, when Ovett informed them that he would only attend their 1980 Sportsview Personality of the Year award programme 'if I am the winner'. In the event Seb, the winner in 1979, was the runner-up to ice-skater Robin Cousins.

❮ It was silly when Steve tried to contrive a pre-Olympic 'challenge' with me when he came back from the States in early 1980. I first heard about it on the radio coming out of Trent Bridge after watching cricket on a Sunday. I'd already agreed with Andy Norman to run for England at Crystal Palace in the Bannister Mile within the England-Belgium-Scotland match because Steve *wanted* the 800 metres. He knew perfectly well that in an Olympic year it would do neither of us any good to get caught up in a really fast race against each other so early in the season. He'd heard I'd pulled out of a race at Loughborough because of a hamstring strain, so he tried to switch to the mile and persuade the AAA, through Norman, that it would be a good thing. It was just sheer opportunism because he happened to be ready earlier. He had already beaten Scott and Bayi, and if he now beat me he could have gone to the Olympics with the psychological advantage of having already beaten the main contenders – though in the event Scott didn't go because of the boycott and Bayi ran the 3,000 metres.

Steve really isn't very shrewd with many of his public comments. When he was asked if he would be going abroad for winter training before the Olympics he said he wouldn't because he was too patriotic! He should try coming to train up in Sheffield or Newcastle in the winter with me or Bren, when you often can't get the car out for days at a time because of the snow. It's not quite like that in Brighton. He has accused me of being a 'programmed' athlete, but every world class athlete has a programme, as he well knows, and mine has been designed to allow me to study at the same time. Often when he makes a comment in public it turns out to be a good omen for me. He said I would never run a fast 800 metres, that the 1980 Golden Mile would be hollow, that he had a ninety per cent chance in the Olympic 1,500 metres, and, after his world record 1,500 metres of 3:31·4 in Koblenz in 1980, that only he and Wessinghage were 'capable of beating 3:30'. I just hoped then that time would prove him wrong! Yet these criticisms relate to comments, and I would never for a moment detract from his enormous athletic talent and exceptional record of racing achievement. In this capacity he has been at the forefront of the resurgence in British athletics. **9**

The circumstances surrounding Ovett's mile record in Koblenz in 1981, sandwiched between Seb's records in Zürich and Brussels in a breath-taking, historic nine days, would be the most bizarre yet – with Scott again at the centre of a controversy in which Ovett appeared to be manipulating the field.

4: Forty-one Days

The winter of 1978-9 was endlessly depressing, an expanse of fog and ice and little daylight, the evenings seeming to begin soon after lunch. For Seb, who had stepped up his winter work to around seventy miles a week for the first time, it required an iron will to maintain his schedules, training early each morning, and again in the evening after a day spent studying for his economics degree. Often he would be running by the light of the moon on snow-covered pavements, foot-paths and lanes, every stride a potential hazard. Only somebody with his extraordinarily detached, clear-sighted view of his objectives could have endured all those hours in which the horizon never came any nearer. One evening towards the end of the winter he was out on a ten-mile run with a couple of Yorkshire colleagues, Malcolm Prince and Andy Armitage. He covered ten miles in three quarters of an hour (the 10-mile world record of Jos Hermens of Holland is 45:57·2), an average of just over 4:30 to the mile, at the end of which he was sick. He went back to his digs, changed, and went to a reception being given by the university warden. After two glasses of wine he felt his legs going, slumped to the floor, and woke up the next day back at his digs where his colleagues had taken him. An Olympic athlete's social life is not a merry one. His April and May appointments were primarily with the 400 metres, working his time down to around 47 seconds in a succession of college meetings, with a relay leg of 46·3. These, you might say, were his 'May Ball'.

❝ My premier aim in 1979 was to get a degree, everything else was subordinate to that. Looking back, 1979 was no different from the year before or the year before that: a reduction in training from March onwards, exams in June, and then a build up of training again afterwards. Peter, George Gandy and I looked at the situation and calculated that if things went well I might get down to somewhere near the pace for a world record

800 metres by the Zürich meeting in the middle of August. I finished exams in the middle of June and caught a virus soon afterwards, probably because I was run down and very tired. Suddenly having nothing to concentrate on, I found myself falling asleep at odd moments and I went to Malmö for the semi-final of the Europa Cup against a background of immensely thorough preparation over many months but in need of sharpening up. It was, in fact, one of the best trips I have ever been on. A lot of senior athletes had turned down the invitation: Geoff Capes, Dave Moorcroft, Brian Hooper and I were the four most senior people there; the team spirit was tremendous, with field events men shouting for the 10,000 metres runners and vice versa. And we were all astonished by the prices out there. After buying a bottle of coke and a tooth-brush I'd just about exhausted the Board's spending allowance for the three days.

I'd withdrawn from a couple of international matches because I knew I just wasn't in the right frame of mind after a month of revising until two or three in the morning for my finals, and only a handful of training runs; but out in Malmö, in spite of its being cold, I found my strength suddenly flooding back, and expending physical energy instead of mental energy was very relaxing. I found I was full of running in the 800 metres, kicking with 200 metres to go and getting home with plenty to spare. **9**

The Board member in charge was Doug Goodman, a large, bland, pleasant man with an unfortunate capacity for malapropisms on a grand scale. In Prague he had wished Brendan Foster good luck when he was lying on the massage table half an hour after he had competed. Now, late into the evening on the Sunday night in Malmö, he was engaged in an attempt to saddle the promoter of the Bislet Games in Oslo, Arne Haukvik, with half a dozen British make-weights. Seb was told he would not be cleared unless the Norwegians would pay expenses for the additional competitors, and it was not until two in the morning that Lynn Davies 'phoned Seb's room to tell him he was free to travel only hours later.

Bislet, nestling near the centre of the city and surrounded by high buildings which protect it from the wind, is an historic setting for countless world records. Over the years some forty have fallen, including many of the most notable. In 1955 Roger Moens of Belgium broke the German Rudolph Harbig's 800 metres record which, at 1:46·6, had resisted all assault for sixteen years. It was here in 1965, in the faint aroma of the nearby Frydenlund brewery, that Ron Clarke of Australia removed no less than 36 seconds from the 10,000 metres record. These, and many other records, had established a tradition which made Oslo the hunting ground of the great, urged on by a knowledgeable crowd who pressed close upon the six-lane track with its tight turns and worn synthetic surface. Yet the youthful Coe was peacefully unaware of most of this as he quietly checked in at the Panorama Somerhotell, high up on the fringe of the city beside the Sognsvatn Lake.

❬ I went out training on the Tuesday in the afternoon, after a loosening forty-minute run on the sandy paths around the lake when I first woke, and a series of warm-up 10 × 150 metres at midday. I was on my own, and after two 400 metres and a couple of 300 metres, I did a series of 200 metres in fractionally under 23. All this was an indication that I was in good shape. Grete Waitz (Norwegian holder of the then women's marathon world record, and European 3,000 metres record) and her husband Jack had been watching, and without my knowing it Jack had also been timing me. He remarked with a smile that I was 'going well'. I felt that I should report the session and back home Peter said 'go out and have a go. Run through the first lap in 50/50·5, then hang on and see what happens.' My own feeling was that if the wind died when the sun went down the next day I might get somewhere near the European record of 1:43·7. That night I went down into the town with John Walker and Rod Dixon, to an English cinema showing *California Suite*. Rod was all prepared for a late night out but Walker's wife was expecting a baby and he wanted to get back to the hotel, and I thought I could do with the sleep. ❭

The next evening Lennie Smith of Jamaica set a fast early pace, closely followed off the first bend by Coe and Mike Boit, but before they reached the 200 metres mark in under 25 it was obvious that something special was happening, because Boit and Evans White of America were already 20 metres adrift. Smith took Coe through the bell in 50·6, and now Coe was on his own, maintaining his rhythm all the way to the tape. Adrian Metcalfe, the commentator for ITV, almost lost his voice as he screamed, 'I don't believe it'. As Coe crossed the line he turned and saw Alan Pascoe, who looked shaken. 'What was it?' asked Coe, barely out of breath. 'Well, I've got 1:42 something' answered the astonished ex-hurdles champion. Walker had watched the race. 'The way he ran was just unbelievable. He looked like he could run under 1:40, he never tied up at all. Seb could win the 800 metres in Moscow and the 1,500 metres in 1984, but he's got nothing to lose by going for both in Moscow.' When Juantorena set a world record of 1:43·5 in Montreal it was supposed that he would dominate the event for several years. But he only succeeded in removing another tenth from that time. In seventeen years the 1962 record set by Peter Snell had advanced less than a full second. Now, on 5 July, Sebastian Coe astonished the statisticians, and caused a ripple throughout athletics around the globe, by lopping a complete second off Juantorena's time with an incredible 1:42·4, more than one and a half seconds faster than he himself had run before.

❛ I had no particular sensation of speed and I think I could have run even faster, I wasn't exhausted at all at the end. I just followed the pace for the first lap which after Prague, as it turned out, was exactly what Peter and I had calculated the optimum would be. All I was thinking to myself was, go on, get stuck in, start working. It was easy. It was the 200 metres after the bell in 24:3 which did it, that was where the record was born. I can remember Dixon and Eamonn Coghlan and Brendan all shouting at the beginning of the back straight. It was a strange feeling – like being on auto-pilot; I was mentally outside what my body was achieving, and it just felt beautiful. But I would have been as happy on the night had I run 1:43·3 as I was with 1:42·4. I found it difficult to adjust to the realization that I was the holder of a world record. The feeling had all been out there on the track. Now I changed out of my running gear to leave the stadium with everyone else, and found that I felt no different. I went and walked round the track alone, to savour the place after the seventeen thousand crowd had gone – and then found I had missed the bus back to the hotel. When I tried to flag down one or two cars going in the right direction they drove straight by. Even

Adrian Metcalfe (former Olympic quarter-miler and now an ITV producer) went straight past without noticing me. Eventually I managed to find a taxi and had what I suppose you might call my first ever real ego trip, when the driver refused the fare. 〉

The entire British press was caught with its trousers down. Such was the modesty of the young man from Sheffield about his intentions in Oslo that none had followed him from Malmö and, with the approach of midnight, all were now left desperately trying to catch up with news from Reuters and the other foreign agencies. Soon the other leading two-lap men around the world were trying to adjust to the news. They would refuse to believe that Coe had not specifically prepared for the attempt, or that he had left the examination halls less than fit barely a month before. Rick Wohlhuter, the Montreal bronze medallist whose 1,000 metres Bislet-run record Coe would lower the following year, insisted: 'It had to be planned, nobody runs that sort of time without.' And former record holder Snell: 'I just hope he hasn't burned himself out a year too early.' Coe, meanwhile, was busy taking two planes, a ferry, and a two-and-a-half-hour car ride to honour a promise to run at a little mining town in northern Norway. He missed all the discussion and, instead, enjoyed himself on some mountain-stream salmon and a gentle 1:51.

〈 I returned from Norway to a normal routine at home, working mainly on speed repetitions in preparation for the AAA Championships, where I'd planned to run the 400 metres. I travelled down to London for the meeting in a state of some alarm as a result of a highly indiscreet and totally unauthorized advertisement placed in *Athletics Weekly* by Mike Tagg of the Viga kit firm. It implied that, following my world record, I sanctioned their goods. Peter and I had to be quick to get hold of David Shaw, the first full-time general secretary of the Board who soon did so much for relations between administration and athletes, to nip that problem smartly in the bud. I ran 46·9 in the heats, easing up, then a personal best of 46·8 in the final, second to Kashif Hassan of Sudan, who went on to win the World Cup. Then it was back to Sheffield, up early on Sunday for a session of repetitions along Rivelin Valley Road, and off to Oslo again. 〉

The first IAAF Golden Mile, launched from the Middle East and scheduled for Tokyo in September 1978, had been cobbled together, largely in London by the West Nally Organization who found the world's best milers reluctant to travel to the Far East at the end of what had already been a hard season. After much persuasion Ovett went to give the event some of the lustre which would otherwise have been absent, and won a slow tactical race, with a kick over the last half lap, in 3:55·5. The American Steve Scott finished a tired fourth behind Gonzales (France) and young Graham Williamson. Only the first three beat four minutes. Scott and his coach Len Miller immediately planned revenge as their target for 1979 in Oslo.

As a result of his invincible running over the previous two seasons, Ovett's attitude in early 1979, publicly at any rate, was that the best mile race in the world ought to come to him at Crystal Palace following his victory in Tokyo. A most laudable view if expressed in the interests of British athletics. By degrees he talked himself into an untenable position for what would turn out to be one of the greatest races ever run. Having decided he could not go to Oslo, he ventured that the race would be hollow without him.

Scott was not the only one who aimed to 'peak' at Oslo. Walker, the Olympic champion who had held the mile record since the memorable first ever sub-3:50 run in Gothenburg in 1975, was anxious to convince the public – and himself – that he was still capable of great deeds. Following the Olympics he had suffered severely from inflamed tendons which had restricted his training, but in January 1979, running at Long Beach, California, he had set a new world indoor 1,500 metres best of 3:37·4. He would defend his mile record in Oslo with his blood. So highly prized did the invitations to this now truly golden mile become, that several notable athletes, among them Moorcroft, the Commonwealth champion, and the young Scot, John Robson, were kept waiting till close to the deadline. It was not until four days before the race that Robson clinched his place by finishing third in the AAA 1,500 metres. Coghlan, winning the AAA 5,000 metres in London with a personal best in a thrilling finish with Mike McLeod, and Dixon, the fastest miler of the year with his 3:52·9 in Philadelphia a month before, would be there.

Because NBC television had bought the rights to the race, it was essential to have an American interest in addition to Scott. So there were Craig Masback, a post-graduate student at Oxford, and Steve Lacy, who had run a 3:54·7 indoors and wanted to be in the race, but who, when most of the runners met at Haukvik's usual strawberry garden party, was reluctant to agree to the requests from Haukvik and Andy Norman to make the pace. So was Williamson, another who had geared his season to this one race. Lacy said: 'I was in a difficult situation over making the pace; of course I wanted to be in the race, but I'd also had a bad throat for five days and considered I could only run to suit myself according to how I felt when I got out there.' Scott, denied his chance for revenge on Ovett, had planned for himself a more clearly defined objective:

'As much as wishing to win the race, I wanted to get that US record of Ryun's of 3:51·1; it was a definite psychological obstacle for me. I knew I was capable of it in the right race, and obviously the race had to be fast. I got together with Thomas Wessinghage, the European record holder, and, on the assumption that somebody would take us through the first half, agreed I'd push it out in the third lap and Tom would try and pick it up for the last quarter.'

Whatever the plans of these two, both Coghlan and Williamson reckoned the man to watch was Coe. So did Walker. Seb himself was into new territory, and uncertain.

Walker's opinion was: 'It's not the Golden Mile for nothing. I've beaten all the athletes here many times. Coe is the question mark, after his 800 metres. He's the danger, nobody knows how good he can be. I just hope that with 200 metres to go I'll be there kicking past him.' Interviewed on television by NBC, Coe had thought, 'it calls for more specialized work than I've been doing'. This would be only his fourth race over four laps in four seasons. He was the most inexperienced in the field and, on paper, the third slowest. Only Bjorge Ruud, a Norwegian, who would set the early pace, and Takashi Ishii of Japan had not recorded a faster mile.

❝ It was an awesome field, with the indoor and outdoor world record holder, the European record holder, the Commonwealth champion, and the second fastest American of all time.

61

Any of them could be the danger. Walker was coming back, getting stronger, Scott was mentally hard, Coghlan had a big kick, but I reckoned Dave Moorcroft might struggle because he was suffering from a bad cold. Peter and I knew the third lap would be critical for someone who was a jumped-up 800 metres runner and not, on experience, a true miler. The record had never entered our heads, to be quite honest I wasn't exactly sure what it was! (I'm always terrible on statistics, and I had made a real ass of myself on a TV sports quiz when I had a mental blockage and couldn't remember who won the 1976 Olympic 1,500 metres.) Our aim was simply to win the race. Something around 57 per lap is six seconds slower than the record 800 metres pace, so it wasn't going to feel too hard at first, but the guys with stamina were going to be coming at me in that third lap. We discussed the race over lunch; I thought it might be tactical but Peter was convinced it would be fast, and said I should get close to the front, stay there, and see how it worked out. **)**

As father and son stood together after the warm up watching the event preceding the mile, the elder man said, 'you can win this'. The younger said, 'I know'. He was feeling good.

At the gun Coe jumped the other twelve runners to avoid the mêlée on the first bend, but Lacy soon took over, leading the runners into the back straight. He'd decided to sacrifice himself as early pace setter because of his weakened condition. Entering the second lap it was Lacy from Scott and Wessinghage, with Coe fourth and Coghlan and Walker bringing up the rear. Down the second back straight Moorcroft and Williamson were still in contention. Lacy's first lap had been 57 exactly, Coe's 57·8. As they came into the home straight for the second time there were still seven or eight of the thirteen in contention. Lacy reached the 880 yards in 1:54·5 and dropped out, and it was now that Scott, closely pursued by Coe (1:55·3), jumped the pack. Into the fifth bend a clear gap had opened with Wessinghage and Coghlan ten yards adrift. Scott, with no sign of Wessinghage and no idea of what was going on behind him, was obliged to drive harder and earlier than he would have wished. It was his effort over the next 300 yards, in the relentless pace of the third lap, which now set up the record and finally killed off all but Seb.

Into the home straight coming up to the bell Coe looked

perfectly relaxed, not a flicker of stress or emotion visible in his face. Fifty yards from the bell he moved to Scott's shoulder: for a moment the American thought it was Wessinghage making his contribution to the last quarter. With a glance behind at the others, now fifteen yards down, Coe made his move. His time at three laps was 2:53, though he didn't hear it, which meant he had covered the feared third quarter in 58. Now he needed fractionally under 56 to break Walker's record. Walker, battling past Coghlan into third place, heard the splits called to the leaders and thought to himself 'it's gone'. Coe started the last lap some three strides up on Scott, who was now the only one near enough to offer a challenge. Walker, with a clear view of Coe's lead around the bend into the last back straight, would say later, 'I was preoccupied with watching him, knowing he was on the way to breaking my record'.

❛ The early pace did not disturb me, but all day I had been worrying about how I would feel on the third lap. I was prepared for it to hurt, but it didn't happen. It was not all that hard. With 600 yards to go I was wondering whether I should go to the front. At 500 yards I looked at the rest of the field and, apart from Scott, saw they were tiring. I was feeling very comfortable, so I stuck in hard for thirty or forty yards, got the gap over Scott, and then began to float. ❜

Around the last lap Coe pulled further away, never straining, while Scott's head went up in the vain effort to stay in touch. 'When Coe went, I should have gone too but I got isolated several yards back with nothing to "key" on. I just didn't know what he did was possible, but I guess it was no surprise to him or his father.' As Coe increased the lead to fifteen yards, passing the 1,500 metres in a European record of 3:32·8, the twenty thousand crowd was going wild with expectation, clapping rhythmically, those at the front hammering on the tin fence separating them from the track. Throughout the lap Coe was continually looking over his shoulder.

❛ I was afraid that someone would come surging up, I

had a nagging doubt that I had done something wrong or unorthodox against a world class field, and that a big kicker would come through. When I looked back twice in the final straight it was fear not pain. **'**

Had he not slowed as he crossed the line, Seb's time would have been faster. Behind him, Scott agonizingly made the same error, eased over the last few yards and missed Ryun's twelve-year-old record by one hundredth of a second. Masback took third, Coghlan fourth, and Robson pipped Walker by half a stride for fifth. Williamson who, but for losing a shoe on the final bend might have got third, was seventh in 3:53·2, two and a half seconds inside Paunonen's European junior record. In this exceptional race the first ten all finished under 3:55·3. As Coe crossed the line there was pandemonium. Peter had sprinted across from the back straight. 'Have I?' asked Seb. 'Yes', said his father, who would add reprovingly later: 'The lesson of the Golden Mile was the one which the first two to finish ignored: run through the tape!'

' I was astonished when Peter said it was a world record, I had no idea it had been that fast. I went on a lap of honour, someone pushed a Union Jack in my hands on the back straight. It was tied to a pole upside down, but that didn't matter just then! It was marvellous to have brought the record back to Britain after twenty-two years, when it was held by another Yorkshireman. **'**

A trail of photographers followed him around the track and Masback, a familiar figure on the British scene who had surprised everyone with his own tremendous finish, observed: 'Seb looked like a combination of the Pied-Piper of Hamelin and Delacroix's *Liberty Leading the People.*' As the Scandinavian summer faded into that beautiful mellow half-light which lasts till next sunrise, the athletes made their way in ones and twos to the customary reception and dinner. Neil Allen of the London *Evening Standard,* for many years perceptive athletics correspondent of *The Times,* reported next morning:

'I'd like the bloke even if he wasn't my father.' With Peter in Pembrokeshire (4 years)

'On your marks' (5 months)

'I think this girl could be fun!' With Miranda (6 and 4 years)

'And in lane one we have an exciting newcomer!' Emma (3) on right, Nick (5), Miranda (9), and Seb (11)

First home, Sheffield Schools 1,500m (14 years)
Sheffield Newspapers Ltd

Sheffield City Schools Cross Country at Graves Park. Aged 13 — and only a year younger than Hallam Harriers colleague Neil Hopkins (behind)
Sheffield Newspapers Ltd

Above: Seb and Peter discuss tactics at Crystal Palace before a Loughborough-Southern Counties match. A scene repeated a hundred times *Bela Domokos*

Below: The breakthrough. Seb wins the 1977 Emsley Carr Mile at Crystal Palace from 1,500m world record holder, Filbert Bayi, in 3:57.7 *Syndication International Ltd*

Leading Steve Scott of America into
the penultimate bend at Bislett, having
just gone to the front in the Golden Mile,
setting a world record of 3:49.0
The Associated Press Ltd

'Someone gave me a Union Jack, it
was upside down, but what did that
matter!' Britain's Golden Miler (1979)
Bela Domokos

All alone at
the finish of
the 1,500m
in Zürich,
with a
third world
record of
3:32.1
(1979)
Popperfoto

'At fourteen I knew
he was good, at
sixteen I had a
strange kind of
certainty that if I
was patient I had a
world beater.'
Happiness, pride,
and satisfaction for
father and son
Bela Domokos

Receiving the
1979 BBC
Sportsview
Personality of the
Year Award from
Sir Roger
Bannister, the
first man to break
four minutes for
the mile
*Syndication
International Ltd*

Posing by the
plaque
commemorating
Bannister's
historic run
Oxford Mail

O.U.A.C
On this track on May 6th 1954
ROGER GILBERT BANNISTER
Exeter College
President O.U.A.C. 1948~1949
ran one mile
in 3 minutes 59.4 seconds
Thus becoming the first man to run
one mile in less than four minutes.

(Left) 'No, I didn't know Ovett thinks he has a 90 per cent chance in the 1,500m!' Seb diplomatically handles a 400-strong international press conference on his second day in Moscow *Popperfoto*

(Above) Father and son in earnest discussion in the Olympic Village prior to the ill-fated 800m final *Popperfoto*

The 800m medal ceremony: Coe (silver), Ovett (gold),
and Nikolai Kirov of Russia (bronze)
The Associated Press Ltd

A different sort of police escort from that in Moscow as
the champion arrives back at London Airport
Syndication International Ltd

'At ten thirty last night, in the restaurant of an Oslo sports club, Sebastian Coe felt the first inkling of what it is like to be regarded as a giant of modern sport. He and his father had arrived late after telephoning Mrs Coe in Sheffield to talk about her son's stunning world record. As the Coes stepped into the room, a treasure trove of Olympic gold medallists and world record holders – men like Ed Moses, Don Quarrie, Miklos Nemeth, John Walker, Rod Dixon, and Brendan Foster – stood and burst into applause. Sebastian stood there looking embarrassed, and then gave a little nod of thanks before busying himself at the self-service counter. Our new record holder is capable of under 3:47, but future times matter little to me today, remembering the incredible sight of Coe running further and further away from his almost mesmerized rivals, until he took his last faltering step.'

As the US *Track and Field News* reported: 'What stunned most observers was his almost complete lack of fatigue after the race. No stumbling, no heavy breathing.'

❦ I felt sorry for John Walker, he was obviously very depressed. Everyone who wanted a photo of me wanted him with me. Even though he'd said he wanted to be in the race when his record went, I didn't envy him, I knew how I'd feel when it happened to me – even though from the start I tried to take the attitude that my records were merely temporary and borrowed. John reacted with great dignity when he received press calls from New Zealand immediately after the race, and said that it was a great occasion and that he was pleased for me. For a while, as with the 800 metres, I found it difficult to grasp what I had done. I was overwhelmed by the compliment which all those other great athletes, including John, had paid me in the restaurant. It really hit me, I suppose, on the 'plane going home when an air hostess came up to me just before we landed in Manchester and asked if I would leave first. When I got out on top of the steps there were about forty photographers on the tarmac, and I thought, wow! I was ushered through customs without having to show my passport. Malcolm Brammer, the sports editor from Radio Sheffield and an old friend, and Peter Cooper of the *Daily Mirror*, had driven over to meet us. They took us home and we found the road was jammed from end to end, with two film crews in the front garden vying for the first interview, and a whole load of photographers who had apparently been there for up to five hours. Eventually I got inside, and for the next few days the family spent most of the time saying I wasn't there – which was true. I was out training to get into shape for Turin and Zürich. **❜**

At the Europa Cup Final in Turin, East Germany carried off both the men's and women's trophies for the third successive occasion. The outstanding individual was Harald Schmid of West Germany with an exceptional double, inside an hour, in the 400 metres hurdles and flat. On the second day Allan Wells silenced the 35,000 crowd in the Stadio Communale with the first defeat of Pietro Mennea by a European over 200 metres for six years, a result which Mennea would reverse in Moscow. The line up for the 800 metres included both Wulbeck of painful Helsinki memory, and Beyer, the thief of Prague, and so gave Seb the scope for a double revenge of sorts.

❜ I could see the headlines if I failed. I'd never before been *expected* to win anything. The prospects frightened me a bit, the realization that for the first time I was running under pressure not for myself but for the team. I wasn't helped by one or two team officials coming up to me and saying that because I was three seconds faster on paper, all I had to do was go out and run from the front – just as if it was a question of driving down to the garage to fill up the car. Peter and I hadn't talked for two weeks. He was away on holiday, but what we had agreed was that it was *unnecessary* to run from the front. Apart from anything else, I was sick to death of so many people during the past year or more saying that I could *only* run from the front and that I could not run without Peter's being there. Even coaches need holidays! I travelled down to the stadium with Brendan and we passed some German supporters chanting, 'Bey-er, Bey-er'. Brendan simply said, 'forget it, go out there and bloody win something for the first time in your life'. It was a friendly, calculated insult, and it was true that the only championship I'd won was the indoor at San Sebastian.

Warming up before the start I refused to look at Wulbeck when he tried to shake hands; I knew that if I accepted his apology for what happened two years previously I would have conceded an advantage. I ran a really cagey race, and was last at the bell. It unnerved those at the front, they were glancing back for me. I moved up to fourth with 200 metres to go, and put in a sprint of 24·4 to finish in front of Zivotic of Yugoslavia with plenty to spare. Wulbeck was third and Beyer fifth. Although the time of 1:47·3 was almost five seconds outside the record, the race did a lot for my confidence. As I ran towards the line I raised my arms in relief, but when I saw it on video afterwards it made me cringe, and I determined not to do *that* again. In the dope-test room I made up a fruit drink from the dispenser for Wulbeck and myself, and we shook hands. **)**

The British press reluctantly returned home from Turin, where Jim Coote's seat in the stadium had remained poignantly empty and a spray of orchids had been put on his desk from the Italian sports writers' association. We left behind the enviable tranquillity of the press club – presented by Fiat millionaire Agnelli – with its tennis courts and restaurants and vast swimming pool, around which in summer are draped some of the city's most elegant ladies, whose husbands pay up to one thousand pounds per annum in order that they may be seen escorting some of the best tans in Italy.

Seb went off to Viareggio for a small-town meeting where he has run for some years – not least because of the all-night Italian knees-up which follows the racing! After this recreational, end-of-season pit-stop, he moved to the Swiss mountain sports training centre at Macolin, high above Lake Neuchâtel. There, he was able to fill his lungs with the pure mountain air and the aroma of pine needles, running free as a deer among the forest paths skirting verdant meadows, with their ample, bell-ringing cows. There is a peacefulness up at Macolin which, in conjunction with first rate physiotherapy and that special brand of comfy, hygienic Swiss hospitality, makes it a haven for sportsmen. Meanwhile, down in Zürich, Andreas Brugger, wealthy promoter of the annual Weltklasse meeting, was busy resisting Ovett's requests to be asked to run in his 1,500 metres. Ovett was told, through Andy Norman, that he could have the 800 metres. Brugger's thinking was that Ovett's inclusion in the 1,500 metres would make it a tactical race and, without having said as much to the Coes, he was looking for another world record from Seb to enhance the stature of a meeting which has been growing yearly. Calculated leaks to the Swiss press meant that by the time Seb arrived down in the crowded, carnival mood of the Nova Park Hotel, it had been established in the public mind that he *was* going for a third record.

     ❬ In particular, an interview with Swiss TV put the pressure on me; the record wasn't something I'd been sitting thinking about up at Macolin. I'd agreed to run in Zürich the previous March. But when the rest of the world *thinks* you've said you will go for it, you're overtaken by events outside your control. Peter arrived from holiday in the Adriatic the same night as me, and told me he'd thought out the lap times for a record *if* the weather was right. We both knew there was a chance for three-in-a-row, which might never come again, but it depended on the weather because we reckoned that I was not going to get too much help from the field. ❭

It was a warm day but close, and as the evening came on a swirling wind got up and an angry sky closed in from the surrounding Alps. As Peter and Seb sat having a coffee following his after-noon sleep, there was the sound of distant thunder; they looked at each other and doubted that it was 'on'. As they walked out of the Nova Park at around 9.00 p.m. to stroll the quarter of a mile to the grass warm-up area, the dust off the pavement kicked up in their faces and, with the increase in wind, it was getting colder. Inside the stadium, Wells had been battling it out with James Sanford (US) and James Gilkes (Guyana) for the IAAF Sprint Championship, running into a two metres per second wind. Wells took the silver medal on aggregate over the two races. From high in the press box we could see the indigo clouds and the lightning illuminating the city. But as the runners came to the line, Seb looking more tense and nervous than in either of the Oslo races, the wind indulgently slackened and the flags on the stadium roof drooped on their poles. Kip Koskei of Kenya went off at a spendthrift pace, immediately imperilling any record, for a first lap in 54·2, with Seb obliged to hold on a yard or so down in a suicidally fast 54·4.

❝ I was very much aware of the crowd and their obvious expectation. Koskei set off at what I knew instantly was too fast a pace, and at the end of the first lap Peter was bellowing at me to slow down. He didn't need to tell me, and we covered the next 400 metres in 59 and were now nearly twenty metres up on Mike Boit. I'd already agreed with Peter before the start, when he'd said, 'it's shit or bust, get out there and hang on'. We'd thought the field might get me through two and a half laps, but with 750 metres still to go I realized I was no longer getting any help from Koskei, so I just had to move in front. I remember suddenly seeing the track empty in front of me as I went by, and knowing there were still almost two whole laps remaining. With an 800 metres time of 1:53, which Peter had yelled at me coming off the fourth bend, I knew the record was there if I wanted it badly enough. I can still today hear the roar from the Swiss crowd as I went in front, and it was that which lifted me. ❞

Seb went through that third lap in a brave 57.6, passing the bell in 2:35·3 and the 1,200 metres in 2:50·8. He had needed 56·9 over the last lap and he did it in 56·8, shaving a tenth of a second off Filbert Bayi's glorious Christchurch run in the 1974 Common-wealth Games with 3:32·03. In forty-one days he had run himself into athletic immortality. No man in history had ever held all three records simultaneously – the 800 metres, the mile, and now the metric mile. Giants of the past, such as Glenn Cunningham, Sydney Wooderson, Jim Ryun, Gunder Hägg, and Peter Snell had held two of the three but never the lot, though Ryun had held the 880 yards in 1:44·9 at the same time as the mile and 1,500 metres in 1967. Coe was the first Briton to hold the 1,500 metres since official International Amateur Athletics Federation records began in 1913, and how the crowd had responded to the lone, frail figure in the British vest as he ran on and on.

❝ I will never forget that draining run to the finish, the crowd were tremendous with their encouragement, and it's the race of which I am proudest in terms of endurance. If I'd had the pacing for longer I'm sure I could have run under 3:30. But immediately it was over I just wanted to get away from the track, anywhere. Physically it had been hard, but the mental exhaustion was total, and when I got back to the hotel room with Peter there was a feeling of colossal anti-climax, an emptiness, and I had no feeling of enjoyment or excitement. I would never want to go through that particular race again. It is difficult to describe the effort it cost me afterwards to go out and do an interview with the BBC, I was in a daze.

Peter flew back to Italy and I stayed a few days in London getting ready for the Rotary Games. I was out training in Richmond Park, being paced by a friend in a car, when we were stopped by the park police and accused of causing obstruction for going too slowly! By the time we had had an argument over something I thought seemed a bit unreasonable, I'd cooled down, and pulled a calf muscle when I started up again, so I missed the Rotary. I went to the meeting and was given a marvellous reception by the crowd which really meant a great deal to me. From the press box I watched Steve have a go at the mile record, but although Peter Browne took him through the half-way on schedule, the third lap lagged. Graham Willamson, who had arrived straight from an eighteen-hour flight from Mexico, where he had won the World Student Games 1,500 metres, just couldn't push out the third lap, even though Steve was yelling 'faster!' in his ear. It was Steve's thirteenth race in five weeks, five of them abroad, and he was simply tired.

When I got home the family was still away. There were so many letters on the door-mat that I could hardly open the front door. My mother and George and I were still answering them in November, and were grateful when the International Athletes Club offered to pay for secretarial assistance. 〉

Among the letters was one from Czechoslovakia addressed simply: 'Sebastian Coe, Great Britain'. Life for the boy from Sheffield was never going to be quite the same again. His one regret of the season was that after the Oslo Golden Mile he had been sent by Sir Roger Bannister the last of a special issue of ties for sub-four-minute milers, and he forgot to wear it when receiving the BBC Sportsview Personality of the Year award in London from Sir Roger.

5: Countdown

❜ During my many discussions with Brendan Foster, he has mentioned from time to time the pressure of well-wishers, weighing down upon him during the eight months or so before the Olympic Games in Montreal. The fact that he couldn't go out to the supermarket with his wife in Newcastle, for instance, without the sixtieth person that day coming up to him and slapping him on the back and saying, 'you're going to bring back the gold medals, aren't you?' Now, in the autumn of 1979, exactly the same was happening to me in Sheffield. I'd have people shouting at me over fences, on passing buses, from halfway up telegraph poles, or out of holes in the ground, not to mention all those in every shop I visited. I went to Hepworth's for my official British suit, and the whole shop stopped work. I must have had seventeen people measuring me all at once, and the look of expectation on their faces, and the knowledge that I would be carrying all that with me and from thousands like them, obviously became a burden. Usually, nothing really bothers me. I suppose I have toughened up a little, and for much of the time that autumn the Olympics might just as well have been July 1981. I've never really felt the pressure of *time*. In the past, when Peter has been wanting to sit down a week or even ten days before a race to work out tactics, I've said 'OK, OK, later'. There's something inside me which never wants to switch on until its absolutely necessary. I didn't feel particularly under pressure from my records, though I was aware of them. The pressure came from people around me, outside the family, behaving unnaturally, constantly worrying about my health where they had never bothered in the past. 'Oh, no, not a cold!' or 'How's the leg?', or '*Do* sit in the back' – from people who you *know* have never before worried about their passenger's seat belt. With that lot, of course, you're not sure whether they are worrying too much or whether they just don't know what to say.

But there is the other lot who are convinced that you must be wanting to go on the razzle every evening, and that *their* working life is infinitely harder than *yours*. They tend to think that just because you're a student at Loughborough you lead a privileged life. They don't realize, and I suppose there is no reason why they should, that you have to get up to go training before lectures and go training again afterwards. I've been out to dinners where everyone is so well meaning that things have dragged on till past 1.00 a.m. when I've wanted to be away by 11.30 p.m. And when I've excused myself – saying I've got to be on the road by 8.00 a.m. – they've looked slightly offended, and have said they've had to be at the factory or market by 7.00 a.m., as if physically it was the same thing. There are always one or two who come up and offer you a cigar, as if they suppose that what you're doing is not *really* all that different from what they are doing. Not that I'm complaining, because many people are very kind, it's just that they don't realize the asceticism of the life one is obliged to lead. I *might* like a brandy, or even a cigar, but that's something which will have to wait. And there are some who are just plain bloody blunt, and say, as if they were being *so* amusing, 'well, if you don't come back with any medals nobody will want to know you'.

There is a tremendous tendency for the public to take you over. In the autumn, after the records, I was due to go over to Telford, only socially, to a grass-track meeting. It was the first time I really realized just what sort of position I was now in. Frank Bough mentioned the event on television, and when I arrived there were 15,000 people or more at a place which wasn't equipped to cope with 5,000. I don't think there were more than a couple of policemen. I'd agreed to autograph some postcard photos, but people started tearing down the tent where I was sitting from all sides, and George Gandy only managed to avoid a nasty situation by announcing that if people sent their names and addresses to Loughborough, we would guarantee to send the cards. That cost us a pound or two in postage! Not to mention the time. To cap it all, Bough had signed off the TV programme by saying, without thinking, 'what an *attractive* young man'. I got the most impossible stick for months afterwards. I couldn't go anywhere without ribald remarks being made. If only people on television realized what one line can do to you. Television is a marvellous medium for reporting the news, for documentaries, and the arts, but it takes gross liberties in its treatment of people's private lives, which is why my family rejected a request to co-operate on *This is Your Life*.

I'd be lying if I said I didn't enjoy a lot of television, watching my favourite club Chelsea play when I cannot get there myself, and it's nice to be able to see my own races on video to check exactly what happened in front of me if I lost, or behind me if I won. I was gratified when I won the 1979 Sportsview award, but there is a tendency for television people to suppose that you *must* be grateful and willing to co-operate in anything *they* decide they want to do.

I've got some good friends in Yorkshire TV, but someone really went over the top after the world records in 1979. A secretary 'phoned to say I was going to be Sportsman of the Year, and would I be there in Leeds in January for the programme. I said I couldn't be as I was going to be out of the country. It was eventually agreed, after persistent messages from the producer Laurie Higgins, that I would go instead to the Leeds studios before Christmas to record an interview, and I arranged a whole weekend around the date. I received a third-hand message at thirty-six hours' notice to say it was off because of a technicians' strike. We next received a message from Higgins saying that it was imperative that I should do the programme after Christmas. I said I was sorry about the union problem, but I had my own problems and could not be there. The next thing we knew there was a film unit in the front garden demanding an interview in our sitting-room. It was a few days before Christmas and we had a house full! Peter told the chap in charge, 'I don't think you've got the message', but he replied, shoving his foot in the door, 'this is going to rebound badly on you'. They left without their interview, and we next had Higgins on the 'phone saying, 'well, if Sebastian can't go to Leeds, what's his coach doing? Who is his coach?' It was all very unfortunate, and the upshot was that the YTV Sportsman of the Year for 1979 was Kevin Keegan!

Although I was still working at Loughborough on a post-graduate degree, I could spread the academic load over two years at my own discretion. In the autumn of 1979, partly because of the social functions which in most instances I found it very difficult to refuse, I spent more time at home. It brought me a lot closer to my younger brother Nick, enabling him to feel that I was really part of the family, not just someone who came home occasionally, took what I wanted and went away again. We had an hour's tennis now and then: I hadn't had a solid hour with Nick in four years and his irrepressible humour was invaluable in the months leading up to the Olympics. I was able to go to a good provincial theatre again, and to see the inside of the Graves Art Gallery in Sheffield. Ironically, with more time on my hands, I watched a lot less television. At Loughborough, because I was always tired after training, I would just slump in front of the telly, which is an atrocious waste of time.

During the last couple of months of 1979 I could easily have eaten three dinners a night – providing I had been prepared to give three speeches. Again, I'm not complaining. I loved my success on the track and the prestige which it brought, the goodwill towards me from complete strangers. But it was clear I would have to get out of the country if I was going to spend the winter preparing properly for the Olympics. Not only would that prevent me from being drowned in goodwill, but I would be able to find somewhere away from the inhibiting cold of northern England. It wasn't that I wanted to be a recluse, just that I needed two or three months of concentrated, uninterrupted training away from the public eye.

With the help of a close friend, Peter and I were able to arrange something that was perfect. From the New Year until March I was able, perhaps for the one and only time in my life, to be a full-time athlete. I'd always been interested in how Steve could train in the morning and then go back to bed until midday, get up and do another run, sleep all afternoon, wake up for another session in the evening, have a meal, and go back to bed. I tried this sort of schedule for a day when I was in Oslo before the mile. Up early, run round the lake, breakfast, back to bed, some striding, sleep after lunch, an evening session on the track at Bislet, back to the hotel for a meal and bed by 9.30 p.m. For one day I was a full-time athlete. I don't want to deride that kind of preparation. It may suit Steve, but temperamentally it didn't suit me. Yet Peter and I knew that to withstand the very special demands of the Olympics, with six or possibly seven races in the space of nine days, I *had* to have a winter working full-time for at least a few months to be able to match other great runners who would be preparing with the same thoroughness. I did it once, yet I doubt if I would ever do it again. **)**

Twenty miles or so to the north-west of Rome on the way to Viterbo, along the winding, fir-lined Via Cassia, just beyond the grand-prix circuit which the Romans call a ring-road, is the sprawling village of Olgiata. The roadside is bordered by the usual cafés and petrol stations, and here and there smart new apartment blocks with expensive landscaped gardens entered by self-locking gates. A couple of hundred yards off the road is one of those large, guarded estates, where the well-heeled, and occasionally the famous, the diplomatic, or the Middle East super-rich come to reside in sanctuary and security, and – equally important – in anonymity, away from the frenetic city. Behind high wire fences are ten square miles of woodland, a rolling golf course, and behind exotic shrubbery, the sort of air-conditioned houses with large picture windows which in England would require a substantial five-figure salary to maintain, let alone to buy. The two entrances are attended night and day, East-European style, by armed guards whose lethargic attitude somewhat belies their instructions to ensure that the unfriendly and unwanted do not gain admittance. There are twenty miles or so of reasonably well maintained private road, the golf course has fairways as wide as St Peter's Square, laid out more with leisure in mind than competition. The club house boasts that kind of casual elegance for which the Italians have no peer – thick carpets on polished wood floors, huge enveloping armchairs and Chesterfields, a bridge room, and a while-blazered bar-man whose bar never closes. In mid-morning you are as likely to see Sophia Loren's mother taking coffee, as an automobile millionaire in Daks plus-fours taking a rather stiff swing on the first tee. The first requirement of membership, apart from your bank balance – which is more stringently selective than any committee – is discretion and good manners. Thus it was that Sebastian Coe was accepted, quietly and almost without notice, throughout the winter of 1979 as he laid the foundations for one of the most rigorous races he would ever run.

Here he passed a hundred days in soothing, gentle sunshine, his limbs cushioned on the rolling grassland or the forest circuit, at times sharing them with gleaming thoroughbreds, their four legs not all that substantially swifter than his two. The only residents who marred his stay were the prowling, aggressive dogs, kept roaming free in their gardens by many of the householders. Fortunately for Seb, the friend's house where he stayed contained only a couple of white cats. There he could be found some lunchtimes, quietly doing the hoovering while the owners

75

were away. He had his jazz tapes, a selection of books, and the flexibility to train not just when he needed to but, more valuably, when he was in the mood. There were days when he felt so good he thought he would never lose another race. The training was perfectly balanced between sessions of lifting anything up to an accumulative total of twelve tons, in weight training at the English school a mile or two down the public road beyond the compound, and the soaring, scorching runs of six or ten miles which would carry him across the golf course almost as fast as a seven iron could drive a ball.

❛ The choice of destination, knowing that I had to get away from England, was pretty narrow in the end. There was the New Zealand-Australian summer circuit or the US indoor circuit, but I didn't want to race, and nor did I want to spend the time talking shop with other athletes. I could have gone to the Finnish training school in southern Spain, but that would have been too public, and I didn't want to stay in a hotel. So it was fortunate that we had friends, whom we had known long before they left England, in Rome. I was able to afford it, travelling to and from the home and paying my way out there, thanks to my sponsorship from the Sports Aid Foundation and Otis. But the greatest value of all of the place, privacy apart, was the intensity, regularity, and quality of the training. I'd run three world records after a low-key winter of appalling conditions and a handful of high-pressure weeks after my exams finished in June. But in Olgiata, for the first time in my life, I was able to organize myself, physically, as I wanted to. I suppose you could say, if it doesn't sound too much like boasting, that I'd run the records on natural talent. Out in Italy I was able to lay the foundations of something much more lasting and permanent. Admittedly, there were some evenings when I couldn't lift my head out of the chair to go upstairs to bed and be ready for the next day's onslaught. But I did see a bit of Rome: some beautiful opera and some very dull Italian league soccer. I did on one occasion slip down to the Olympic Stadium for a bit of a work out, and it was lovely to be back on a track again. There was the temptation to let rip, but that could have been damaging and might have attracted the attention of some passing journalist, so I just played it cool, did some striding, and then disappeared back down the Via Cassia. Certainly I was tired a lot of the time, but there is so much more value in training without mental stress from the hassle of other activities. And when I wasn't tired, I was able to start reading for pleasure again for the first time in years. *❯*

At intervals Peter flew to Rome to monitor the training and the progress of *his* thoroughbred.

'The records didn't really affect our preparation for the Olympics. What they had given us was confirmation that our methods were right, plus the knowledge that Seb had more natural talent than we had supposed. What we needed now in training was the same, only more so. For the first time we could enter a track season with a whole winter of unbroken preparation. The only slight difference out at Olgiata was a concentration on stamina, because of the packed Olympic schedule. The build-up on speed would come on the early season track, mainly with a series of 800 metres. By the time he came back to England, Seb would have to meet a series of targets in training sessions on the track.'

On Easter Monday, his friends having returned home to England on holiday, Seb carefully put away the crockery in the kitchen, packed his tapes and his running shoes and, after a vain search for the cats, said good-bye to his oasis of the last three months. As we turned the corner at the top of the road, heading down towards the main gate of the compound, we observed that the cats, too, had gone away for the week-end, and were enjoying the sun in a neighbour's garden; they had their own back door entrance. The next hour or so was something like Rimsky-Korskakov's 'Flight of the Bumblebee' as we buzzed our way round the ring-road, overtaken and overtaking on both sides, to pick up the Autostrada del Sol to Florence and Milan, where Seb was due to run in a specially organized road race at the little shoe-manufacturing town of Vigevano. Once on the freeway, where we discovered the toll-keepers were all taking the day off, it was a glorious run through undulating Tuscany under a forget-me-not-blue sky. Pausing for a cup of tea at a service centre outside Bologna, we were offered the usual cut-price trousers and fur coats by unshaven Yugoslavians. Losing our way south of Milan when leaving the autostrada, we arrived late in the evening to find Peter *agitato*.

I wasn't sure who looked the more fretful, he or the Italian organizers of the race, having had visions, no doubt, of their would-be champion somewhere in a ditch beside the road. Seb had, in fact, telephoned to advise his hosts that he might be late, and quietly took his father on one side to release some of the steam before a gasket was blown. The next problem to be overcome was the fact that the race had been routed through and round this beautiful fifteenth-century town, with its inspiring Leonardo da Vinci main square, so that most of it was over cobble-stones! Three months' work could be undone in a quarter of an hour. Peter and Seb, having inspected the course by moonlight, stated that if it could not be altered he could not run. With the entire population, down to the newest babe in arms, scheduled to turn out to watch in a little over twelve hours' time, with the bunting already marking the course, which would be specially closed to all traffic, and with the mayor and the chief of police already in bed, and unlikely to rise early enough to sanction a last minute change, the organizers looked as if they might burst into tears. However, the nation renowned for its resourcefulness in fixing things duly did so, and on a lovely day Seb coasted clear of a field that included international road runners, to enter the square at the finish like some Sir Galahad, to a huge ovation. Even the *carabinieri* clapped. Hardly breathing after five miles in under twenty-five minutes, Seb put on his tracksuit and went looking for some shampoo before meeting the mayor for lunch.

Back home in Yorkshire he had an appointment of considerable significance with physiologist Professor John Humphreys at Leeds Polytechnic, where he was to be subjected to every imaginable test in order to measure the effect of his winter's work. They stuck a long rubber tube in his mouth, sellotaped electrodes to all his arterial signal boxes, put him on a tread-mill, and told him to start running – in order to measure the efficiency of oxygen uptake and pulse-rate in relation to pace.

6 After twenty to twenty-five minutes the machine was beginning to smoke and so was I! Neither of us could go any faster, and I was doing around twenty miles an hour. Put simply, the results told me that my winter's work had been more valuable

78

than ever before. ❱

Humphreys, who felt obliged by the results to check his apparatus, was able to reveal that Seb now had an oxygen efficiency equivalent to the top marathon runners, and suggested that whereas normal athletes had one gear and outstanding athletes two gears, Seb, physiologically, had three. Armed with this knowledge, with the evidence of the previous year's records, and the logical projection of his latest training onto performance on the track, Seb sat back with me one afternoon to make an objective assessment of his Olympic prospects in his two distances. His calm, almost detached conclusions, as realistic as an astronaut accepting without question that NASA has got its sums right, were frighteningly emphatic.

'In the 800 metres I don't think there is really a serious challenge. No one. James Maina of Kenya might be a medallist if the Kenyans go. He is 1·5 seconds slower on paper, which may not be much physically but, at that sort of pace, it's considerable physiologically. If the race is fast, there will be nobody else who knows what it's like under 1:43. I've been there before, and I know it doesn't hurt, and that I'm in better shape than last year. I think there are one or two who will give Steve some bother in the 800 metres if it's fast. In the 1,500 metres it *should* be between Steve and me. I think Masback and Scott (if the Americans go), and Coghlan and Straub will be in for third place.'

We were sitting in my garden. Seb had allowed himself the rare treat of a Campari as we idly watched George the tortoise making tracks for his favourite resting place, between runs, among the roots of a fir tree. Although I had become accustomed over several years to Seb's realistic assessment of any situation, this forecast, which I agreed with basically, took my breath away when stated so baldly. To be that *certain* in your own mind was to carry around a responsibility to yourself which could be unnerving.

❰ It is possible to psyche yourself up for something without really believing it deep down. But if you genuinely do believe it, there's no hiding from it. It's like breaking a stick of rock and finding the writing's the same all the way through. It's a far worse situation to be in, knowing that you have to do something stupid *not* to win a race, than thinking that you will have to do something startling if you *are* to win it. There was nothing, including Steve, that I'd seen at either distance which worried me. **'**

I immediately began to conceive of him winning the 800 metres, running from the front in the most dramatic fashion like Bayi in the Commonwealth 1,500 metres. What about it? The idea appealed to him, but he and Peter had already discussed tactics, with two months still to go, and had arrived at a basic plan, more or less similar for both races: that he would sit in on the leaders, never allowing himself to get out of touch, and strike, Ovett-style, in the last 150-250 metres, on the basis that, whatever the pace of either race up to that point, he could not be 'dropped'; and that whatever the remaining portion of the race, he could cover it faster than anyone else still in contention. It was a fail-safe approach, used so devastatingly by Ovett in over forty consecutive races. But how would he cope with the temperamental shock of coming away with defeat in one, or both, races?

'It would be a disappointment, but it would only last until the next time I had to go out for a racing performance. That is not to say that I do not desperately want to do well. I do. I want to succeed very much, simply for the work I've put in, and which Peter has put in, and for the effort of my family. But if it doesn't come off I won't walk through the rest of my life a failure. I would know I had failed at that time, but I could accept honest failure – being beaten on the day by someone who has proved himself the better man. That is the name of the game. I remember listening to the radio on the morning of the 1974 F.A. Cup Final, and hearing Alec Stock, the Fulham manager, saying 'Some players will wake up feeling it's just another day, others that they will end the day with blood on their boots.' That's how I hope it will be with me. That if I fail, I will do so having given my best.'

In the light of events, they were to prove poignant words. At that stage it was by no means certain that Britain would be going to the Olympics. The government, led by Mrs Thatcher, was making repeated requests to individual athletes and to the British Olympic Association chairman, Sir Denis Follows, to stage a voluntary boycott of the Games, in line with American policy as laid down by President Carter – and reluctantly accepted by US sportsmen and women. While the argument raged, and the elderly but adamant Follows was twice summoned to Downing Street without yielding, Seb adroitly sat on the fence. This was not indecision. He understood the dilemma perfectly, and had not yet made up his own mind. I had by then given my personal opinion in the columns of the *Daily Express*: Britain was wrong to send teams either to South Africa – the Lions rugby team – or to Moscow. I well knew, after extensive travelling over twenty years in every Eastern European country including Albania, the extent of the erosion there of personal liberties which every man and woman in Britain takes for granted. I had friends behind the Iron Curtain whose experiences were appalling, but I was careful not to attempt to put any pressure on Seb, whose position was utterly different from mine. Privately, I felt it would be a noble gesture if he withdrew, knowing his confidence in his success, but it was in no way my position to influence him. Regarding my own *practical* involvement, I considered that, as in war, the journalist must suspend his own moral views in the matter, and go and report the facts. Having gone, the facts merely strengthened my existing views on the inhumanity of the Russian régime, but they altered my view on the boycott.

With hindsight, I believe that the West should have flooded Russia with as many visitors as possible, to make as much contact as possible with ordinary Soviet people in order to strengthen their resolve in their quest for the freedom of thought and speech and work and travel which they are denied. Seb was in a much more difficult position as a prominent international sportsman, knowing that the premature public expression of any decision he made would be used as an implement of persuasion by those whose view he supported. He did not wish to be the public Litmus paper. Even so, some innocuous remarks made to Alan Hubbard, the sports correspondent of *Now* magazine, were picked up by the Russian Tass news agency, twisted, and distorted into a personal attack on Mrs Thatcher. They were reproduced by, of all papers, the *Daily Telegraph*. It was doubly irritating, because he had leaned over backwards to retain a neutral public front. As an intelligent, articulate man with a degree in economics, social history and political science, he, less than most, needed to be told what he should think. Ultimately he decided in favour of supporting the action of the British Olympic Association, and he accepted his invitation.

❝ When I decided to go, some people accused me of being a Communist. Nothing could be further from the truth. Every athlete has political views, but I do not believe personal politics should influence one's decision on such a vital issue. I thought about the matter of Afghanistan at great length and initially I would say I was sympathetic to the government line. I believe that you have to support the elected government, whatever your own political views. That's democracy. Parliament had voted heavily in favour of not sending a team, and on other issues I would certainly argue that we should not go against Parliament. But by degrees I became disenchanted with the government's *attitude*. Without consulting any sports body, such as the Sports Council, and with no knowledge of, or real interest in, international sport, the government suddenly sent the Foreign Secretary to Lausanne to discuss an alternative Olympics – without any kind of feasibility study. I considered it was an insult, that with a national budget for sport of some fifteen million pounds, it was suddenly possible, at a stroke, to find fifty-five million pounds for an alternative Olympics in London. I came from a city where there was not even a single all-weather running track, and I regarded the government's attitude as totally political rather than strategic.

I was also anxious that any government, Conservative or Labour, should not initiate sporting sanctions for some short-term political pay-off. After that, nothing in sport would have been sacred, and international sport – the World Cup in soccer or anything else – would have been placed in an impossible position. *If* the government recommended a package which included trade, cultural, and social boycotts as well as sporting ones, I would not have been happy but I would have supported it. But to select just two hundred international sportsmen and make them a persecuted minority was the cheapest form of political one-upmanship. Nor did you have to be particularly astute politically to realize that America and West Germany, the two main western countries

82

favouring the boycott, were involved in elections, and the existing leaders, Carter and Schmidt, were faced by right wing opponents Reagan and Strauss. In both instances the leaders were probably looking for some political focus, and I didn't feel we should get caught up in this political stunt. Of course I had sympathy for Afghanistan's plight, and with that of Hungary and Czechoslovakia in the past, but I needed to be sure that any action on my part was going to make some difference. And I do not think one should overlook the point made by Enoch Powell: that the government could not compel unless they had the will of the people, or an act of legislation, and they had neither. The country was split 70-30 against the boycott. **'**

Seb's early season build-up on the track was quiet and relatively inconspicuous, a 3,000 metres here, a 1,500 metres there, a 5,000 metres in the Yorkshire Championships at Cudworth in a bitterly cold wind where he ran outside fourteen minutes. But towards the end of May he began to sharpen, with a 1:45·4 in the Inter-Counties and, on 5 June, a 1:44·98 for Loughborough against the AAA, on cinders. This was followed by a 1:44·7 in the Northern Counties. All satisfactory, on the face of it, but what the public did not know what that he was beginning to be severely troubled by a sore hamstring – the result of something even more critical: sciatic nerve trouble due to fractional displacement of the pelvic girdle over a long period.

' It had been troubling me on and off in the first few races of the season and on 14 May, following Cudworth, I'd had to pull out of a Loughborough match at the moment I was warming up before the race. It was four days after this that Steve issued his 'challenge', while he was running down in Wales, for the meeting at Crystal Palace on 21 May. The outcome of all that, inevitably, was that we switched events, he ran the 1,500 metres, I ran the 800 metres. The injury was beginning to be rather disturbing, only weeks away from Moscow. I'd originally had treatment back in 1979, before the records, from Terry Moule, the osteopath who got Gerry Francis playing again for Queens Park Rangers, and who sorted out the back problem of Roger Uttley, the England rugby forward. Terry believes that in the main all muscle problems have a structural beginning, unless they are sprinters' pulls or collision injuries. He'd already talked of my having a tilt of the pelvis. On and off in June, I was also having treatment from Eddie Franklin, the 'physio' at Chelsea, who was doing a fine job of keeping the hamstring flexible. I played quite a lot of tennis with Ian Hague over a couple of months at this time, and had difficulty stretching for low balls. By the beginning of July it was beginning to cross my mind that I might not make it to the Games. **>**

On 27 June, running in the Talbot Games at Crystal Palace, Ovett took over the 1980 world rankings for 1,500 metres with a time of 3:35·3, the fourth fastest of his career. He was hard pressed down the finishing straight by Steve Cram, whose 3:35·6, at nineteen years eight months, was the world's fastest by a teenager. A few days later the two great British rivals, Ovett and Coe, set off for Oslo and the Bislet Games. In what had been a bid for Coe's 1,500 metres record at Crystal Palace, Ovett had been unsuccessfully paced by Bob Benn and Britain's third Olympic 800 metres runner, young Dave Warren from Essex. Before Oslo, Warren had told John Rodda of *The Guardian* and me that he would not agree to pace Ovett again in the Bislet Mile, but when we arrived at the Panorama Hotel it was to discover that pressure had been put on Warren by Andy Norman to make the pace once again.

Coe was going for his fourth world record, the American Wohlhuter's 1,000 metres. I knew of his hamstring problem, which I had not disclosed, and I knew likewise of an exceptional 600 metres in training. For the first time, too, Angela would be there to watch her son in a world record bid. On another glorious Norwegian summer evening both runners delivered the goods. Seb had selected the 1,000 metres to make it a unique four-in-a-row, from 800 metres to the mile, and his first question when I met him at the airport, where I had arrived from a meeting in provincial Norway the previous day, was, 'what's the programme tomorrow?' I was able to tell him that his race was the earlier by an hour, so that even if Ovett was now successful in his bid for he mile, Seb had the chance to be the possessor of all four records for that hour. On the morning of the race we had a stroll around the lake, and Seb explained that his intention was to run the first 800 metres fast and then hang on, rather than save anything for the final 200 metres and finish the race not having expended everything. Wohlhuter's 2:13·9 was considered a 'hard' record; he had passed the 800 metres en route in 1:46·8, and Seb was now aiming for something around 1:46. Although he had eased the problem in his leg for the moment, he was still suffering from the after effects of a heavy cold and throat infection, for which he had been taking antibiotics, and had had to cancel a race in Sweden the previous week.

The start was ridiculously fast: Mike Solomon, Trinidad's Moscow 400 metres representative, went off at such a pace that Bob Casselman, the American hurdler who had been put in by the organizers to take the first leg, could not even get to the front! Solomon went through the 400 metres in 50·1, and Coe in 51, which was pace for an 800 metres record, never mind the 1,000 metres. With a lap to go Coe was out on his own, thirty metres ahead of his old rival Wulbeck, needing a 56 to break the record. He went through the 800 metres in 1:45·2 (the fourth fastest time of the year!) and was now in trouble with his breathing, with Wulbeck gaining ground. Coe gritted his teeth and, looking more strained than in any of his previous three records, held on for his fourth in 2:13·4, with Wulbeck still ten yards down. As he set off on a lap of honour, he shared with Rono a rare distinction of a 'simultaneous' quartet.

❝ I was pleased, because I wasn't well. In a way it was harder than running a hard 1,500 metres. We only decided finally to go for the record once we knew that Maina wasn't in the field, and we decided to make it fast for the first two laps because physiological information we had about Wulbeck, from tests in Germany, suggested he would find it hardest that way. I didn't hear the 800 metres time, but I knew from the pace Solomon had set that it must be quick, and that I would really have to start working over the last 200 metres. I tied up badly between 130 and 80 metres out, and then I managed to get fluid again. But for the cold I think I could have run 2:12, but at least I'd done it with my mother watching. I'd given her a little something back for all those months and years of patience and attention she had given me. As I ran the lap of honour, I could see her up in the stand sitting next to John Walker's wife. For a few hours afterwards my system was really turned upside down, I was very sick. Whatever doctors say, antibiotics affect your system physically. But however grotty I was feeling temporarily, it was a good finish to my Olympic preparation. 〉

It was with rare expectation that the Bislet crowd awaited Ovett's appearance. They were not disappointed. Warren took the field through the first quarter in 55·5, with Ovett slotted in behind. In fourth and fifth position Steve Cram and Graham Williamson were locked in a duel to decide which of them would be Britain's third runner in the Moscow 1,500 metres, one of the last vacancies in the track and field team. Warren led Ovett through the half-way mark in 1:53·5, and Williamson, who throughout the season was beset by one misfortune after another, had already fallen away. Ovett's two-lap time of 1:53·8 put him one and a half seconds ahead of Coe's pace in the record run the previous year; and a 57 third lap left him no less than 2·4 seconds in front of Coe's time at the same stage. Warren had dropped out with 600 metres to go, obliging Ovett to go to the front. Looking in superb shape all the way to the tape, Ovett was home in what seemed to be a new record. But was it?

Unaccountably, for the only time in more than twenty races in the meeting, the electronic timing apparatus had stalled. It was said later that the starter's gun had failed to activate the clock, so the judges were dependent on the back-up timing of hand-held watches. After a long delay the time was announced as 3:48·8, a fifth of a second inside Coe's record. But would electronic timing, always considered to be fractionally faster in activation and therefore producing a slower time, still have given him the record? The many international journalists present debated the matter into the early hours of the morning. What was certain was that, under IAAF regulations then in force, Ovett's time would be recognized – and that he and Coe were heading for one hell of a confrontation in Moscow.

〈 Of course I was disappointed, but I wasn't shattered; I didn't feel I'd lost a part of me, and it wasn't quite the blow I'd felt it had been to John Walker the previous year. I watched with Peter, and when 2:51 came up for the three-quarter mile, he thought Steve would really rupture the record by a couple of seconds. Steve and I had a brief talk afterwards, I told him I'd enjoyed his race and he thanked me but said he hadn't seen mine because he was warming up. As far as I was concerned, it was irrelevant who held the record when it came to the Olympic 1,500 metres. The record was only borrowed for Steve, the same as it was for me. People questioned me indirectly after Steve's record in the following days, as much as to say, 'what are you going to do about that?' But I never doubted that he was capable of it, I was sure he had been for some time. What mattered to me, at that stage in Oslo, was my own confidence in winning in Moscow, whether the 1,500 metres was run at 3:37 pace or 3:28. I was encouraged by the fact that both Walker and his coach Arch Jelley told me they felt I would win. **〉**

Adrian Metcalfe was less certain. His closing message to ITV viewers back home in Britain was, 'well, I leave you with a comparison of the last 200 metres of the two races, and ask yourself who is looking the easier . . . ' Two weeks later Ovett returned to Bislet for yet another record attempt, this time on Seb's 1,500 metres mark, with the Olympics less than a week away. He now stoked the flames even higher for the meetings in Moscow by equalling Coe's record. This time the electronic clock was working, and Ovett crossed the line at the end of a fierce race with Wessinghage, Walker, and Lacey, in 3:32·09. That was six hundredths of a second slower than Seb's Zürich record, but both rounded up to the same 3:32·1. If neither improved on their times before the IAAF introduced records measured to a hundredth in January 1981, Seb's would stand as the faster. The two remarkable Britons entered the Games with two records each and one shared: Seb the 800 metres and 1,000 metres, Steve the mile and two miles, the 1,500 metres held jointly; the prelude to a riveting showdown.

〈 I wouldn't have wanted a race so close to the Games, it was a break from training routine for Steve at a time when training was in my opinion more important. He claimed he wanted the psychological advantage of it. Things were brewing up for a good series of races in Moscow. **〉**

6: A Race Without History

A rainbow of flags, like balloons at a children's party, fluttered from every lamp post, beckoning us to suspend all thought of reality. Once we had run the gauntlet of unsmiling immigration inspection, we were expected to be seduced by Moscow's lavish party, so much of it as artificial as the cardboard wedding cake in the baker's window. The 1980 Olympics, once they began, were, as always, made by the athletes, not by the city in which they happened to be. As one walked through the Village gates once more, Baron de Coubertin's now almost extinct ideology of *taking part* was still there in the air, a concept which, however much it may have been eroded by politics, professionalism, and the use of drugs, still carries faintly the old alchemy of a common pursuit of excellence. Of course, in one sense, the whole thing was a stupendous absurdity, a giant stewpot of vested interests in which the Killanin-led administration was dwarfed and overrun by its own vehicle. Yet, although the 1979 Soviet Government official handbook for Party Activists might claim, 'to decide to hold the Games in Moscow is convincing proof of the recognition of the correctness of our country's foreign policy', there would be few competitors who would believe this preposterous claim for a moment.

There were many visitors to the Games, including competitors, who came and went without ever sensing or seeing the dark side of Soviet life. The city had been laundered for the occasion. Dissidents, drunks, most cars, and children under sixteen had been evacuated, their places taken by the thousands of extra police who hovered every five yards on every street, even hiding in the bushes, ensuring that there was the minimum contact between the ordinary Russian and any visitor from the West. The hundreds of officials required to administer the Games, from stadium stewards to waitresses, would not fraternize one jot beyond the formal necessities of doing their job – which is not to say that in most instances the job was not done exceptionally well. That is why some unquestioning visitors left with the impression that the Russians have the sun shining out of their hearts. Sadly, that is precisely the point. Many of them do, but they are bound, in every action they take, by the most comprehensive totalitarian régime ever known to man. By the time the three weeks were drawing to a close, some of the formality had melted. Off duty, unobserved in the back of a bus with his beret off, the Russian 'squaddie' was no different from one anywhere else in the world: interested in a chat, a beer, a laugh, a fag, and a pretty girl. I know because I met them. It was the same with the translators in the hotels and press centres, with the concierges who monitor every floor of every hotel, enthroned like plebeian Queen Victorias behind their desks, dispensing room keys and tea at any hour of the day or night and, in consequence, all-seeing. But beneath an adopted severity many of them were as gentle as any granny. It is the system, not the human beings who comprise it, which is depressing – show your identification to pass through every door, to mount every bus; if you go out of the hotel front door to speak to a colleague standing on the pavement, return by *another* door through electronic scrutiny back into a hotel where there is nobody but journalists anyway! 'Marry me', said a hostess in the Lenin Stadium press centre with a sardonic laugh, as she chastely handed me the latest information sheet from the computer, 'and I promise to leave you the moment I step foot in London!' She, and a million others.

❝ As we came in to land, the British Airways pilot said over the intercom: 'Ladies and gentlemen, we are about to arrive in Moscow. Enjoy yourselves!' There was a wave of laughter. As we taxied in, you could see line upon line of civil aircraft, as if the Russians were anxious to show us their new prosperity. We came into the vast, empty arrival hall, like some huge cardboard cut-out, soulless in its emptiness. There was all hell let loose the other side of customs. As we boarded a bus, Alan Pascoe put an arm round me and said, 'well, I hope you can get some peace and quiet now you're here'. I don't think he realized the irony of that. Daley was lapping it all up as usual, adoring the attention. As we left the plane, a stewardess had given me a couple of plastic bags of mini tins of orange juice. Daley had grabbed them, saying he needed them for his ten events, Brendan joked that he could get a house for them in Moscow. We were the usual happy, laughing bunch of sportsmen arriving before a big event. Brendan was a bit smug that he was no longer the centre of attention, that he wasn't obliged to perform for the cameras.

I had set off prepared for the same as in Prague: to queue in Moscow, to have to wait for food, and not to be all that happy. But once I arrived in the Village I was very impressed with the rooms, and the space, though there was more room in the Village, in terms of the accommodation, because of the boycott, of course. The security was oppressive, but you just had to bear with it, and they'd painstakingly searched all my books at the airport. The food turned out to be superb, huge amounts of everything you could want: steaks, fish, fruit, cereals – most of it imported, of course – and one heard that the Russians had gone without many things in the preceding months so as to provide for the Games. The East Europeans had clearly seen nothing like it for ages, you'd see Bulgarian weightlifters leaving the self-service counter with whole trays of oranges and bananas. It was a pleasant surprise to find that the living conditions were not going to be a hassle.

My preparation had gone as well as I could have hoped; apart from the hamstring I was as fit as I'd ever been. It was Sunday, I wasn't racing till Thursday, and I could relax a bit. Yet there was also a strange, almost hollow feeling, knowing that for the duration of the Games, for the next two weeks, this was your world, you wouldn't be going anywhere else other than to the Stadium, and that at the end of the two weeks all the speculation and questions would be answered. I found myself looking at people and wondering how they would react, what they would be saying to each other if I came away with nothing. In the artificial surroundings of a Village, you cannot be yourself, on your own: whether you like it or not you are thrust upon other people to an extent, and they on you, and you start getting caught up in their feelings, the way I suppose it must be among the crew of a submarine. **)**

The only practical irritation on arrival had been that British

Airways had given substance to the apocryphal slogan 'Breakfast in London, Lunch in Moscow, Luggage in Tokyo' by losing a grip containing all Seb's training gear. Luckily his running spikes had been in a small bag which he never allows out of his sight. While BA went hunting – 'Hello, is that Siberian lost property?' – Seb hurried off to the most heavily attended press conference in the history of the Olympics. It was the intention of David Shaw that such a conference would give the world's press the opportunity to question the triple world record holder at the first available moment, and thereafter allow him some peace. Interest in the Rossiya Hotel – a self-contained block the size of Green Park, with 6,000 beds, where the entire written press was housed in 'quarantine' away from the locals – had been fuelled by Ovett's interview two days previously, in which he had stated that he had a fifty per cent chance in the 800 metres and a ninety per cent chance in the 1,500 metres. But the gathering of 400 or more press and TV men was kept waiting in the main press centre lecture room in central Moscow for over forty-five minutes.

The cause of this delay was symptomatic of the red tape which was to drive some of us almost to resignation in the coming weeks. Because neither Seb nor Peter were accredited journalists, they required, believe it or not, elaborate separate accreditation to enter the press centre! And the authorities had got themselves in a twist over Peter and Percy. Peter's real name is in fact Percy, duly entered in his passport, but some sharp-nosed bureaucrat had spotted that his Olympic accreditation was in the name of Peter. Ah, zo, a plot! It took almost an hour for the error to be acknowledged as such, corrected, and approved, after which the world's foremost athlete and his coach were at liberty to meet the press. Seb, reasonably relaxed, tactfully deflected barbed questions. No, he wasn't under instructions not to answer political questions, his views were already well known and he was now here exclusively to run. Yes, he was pleasantly surprised with the Village and the excellence of the food. Yes, he would definitely run both the 800 metres and the 1,500 metres, contrary to rumours going round the press hotel. No, in answer to an East German, he did not think he and Ovett would be running as a team! No, in answer to Ovett's allegation that he was a 'programmed' athlete, his training was not that hard and was less than that of some others. Yes, he hoped Bayi would be in good shape for the 1,500 metres, 'because we want it to be a fast race of which we can all be proud'. Did Ovett really think he had a ninety per cent chance in the 1,500 metres; if he did he must have a crystal ball. No, in answer to a Finn, he had no detailed knowledge of the East German or Soviet runners, but he didn't prepare for races with individuals in mind. No, he wasn't worried by Ovett's recent records, he had always believed Ovett had the ability. Tass, the Soviet news agency, asked enigmatically what his feelings were as a human being, now he was in Moscow. Seb, equally enigmatically, said he felt 'an element of excitement'. Didn't we all!

❛I was a little bit worried that I would give the impression that I was holding court, doing an Ali, which was exactly what a German asked: 'Why are you here?' But looking back, the press conference was a good thing and when I went to the training track that afternoon I was able to say to journalists who wanted to interrupt that I had already answered all the questions I was able to. The British team officials Nick Whitehead and Lynn Davies, kept off the photographers.

I hadn't heard about Steve's prediction till I arrived at the press conference. We travelled on the Sunday and I missed the papers. My first thought was, is he confident or insecure? What *are* the implications when you suddenly open up to a newspaper after systematically refusing to talk to the press for several years? He could have said what he said to any of the regular athletics writers, and he would have received good coverage, so when he suddenly talked to a paper which does not normally give much attention to athletics, you have to wonder why. Apart from any other consideration, his exclusive interviews with a Sunday paper and with ITV were contraventions of the Olympic charter, which states that while a competitor is not obliged to give interviews, if he does he should be available to all sources. I was left with the feeling that he had probably been used, that his feelings had been overstated for the benefit of the paper's 'exclusive'. In fact, Steve and I were on very good terms in Moscow. We had sympathy for each other, knowing that the eyes of the world were on us, that it was some kind of Judgement Day, that whether or not we both won gold medals people would make distinctions and overload them upon us. I have a tremendous respect for his athletic ability, he is one of the most talented runners there's ever been, and his range, from 400 metres to a half-marathon, is unsurpassed.

The days leading up to the heats of the 800 metres were uneventful. I was relaxed, sleeping soundly, moving well on the track, and the hamstring was easing. I felt my condition was improving with every day I was there, my heavy cold from Oslo had cleared, and the sun was doing me a power of good – I was delighted when it really became scorchingly hot the day before the 800 metres heats. I was conscious of pressure, but at this stage it was an abstract thing. I'd felt it most, in a strange way, when I went down with Peter to inspect the track; standing there in the empty Lenin Stadium, where the action would all happen, for the first time I suddenly began to grasp the enormity of the occasion. Yet I liked the track, it was not too hard, the curves were good, the whole place had a mood of drama even when empty. All in all, I felt confident that I could cope with whatever was thrown at me in the next few days. Speed hurts, sustained speed kills, on the track; and from my experience of the world records at 800 metres and 1,000 metres, I felt that I could, if necessary, sustain something faster than anyone else **❜**

By the time the six 800 metres heats were completed, the thought crossed my mind that the East Germans were in a possible position to run a team race in the final. Andreas Busse, Olaf Beyer (the Prague champion), and Detlef Wagenknecht (referred to among the British as Wagon Wheels for simplification) were all tall and powerful, and it was certainly on the cards that they could make a team decision as to who had the strongest individual chance, and then get the other two to gang up on the British, tactically. Busse, second to Seb in the rankings prior to the Games, looked particularly impressive, as did Nikki Kirov, the powerful little Russian in a blood red vest. Ovett began the saga with an untroubled 1:49·39 in the opening heat, then came Wagenknecht and Kirov with a joint 1:47·5, followed by Busse with 1:47·34. Seb, coasting wide in fourth place at the bell – 'like running in a greenhouse', as Mike McLeod, Britain's 10,000 metres runner, said – had an easy 1:48·43, marginally faster than Beyer in Heat Five, with Dave Warren comfortably home in the sixth and slowest heat. With the first three from each heat and the six fastest among the losers qualifying for the three semi-finals, it had been simple enough for the fast men. The semis would be tougher, with only the first two and the two fastest losers reaching the final. The draw put Seb in the third semi, with only 'Wagon Wheels' likely to offer any challenge to him at that stage.

❢ There was no problem: I was relaxed, ran wide down the first back straight to keep out of trouble, was nicely placed in third position at the bell, and pulled ahead of Wagenknecht in the last 70 metres, after holding onto his surge round the final bend. We were given the same time, and I now felt that he was the main threat amongst the East Germans. Beyer had unexpectedly gone out in the second semi, fourth behind Kirov, Dave Warren, and Marajo of France. My time, and Kirov's and Steve's in the first semi, were almost identical, and my feeling about the final was no different from before the Games started. I considered I was sufficiently improved to cope with whatever cropped up, leaving aside the fact of my record being a second faster than anyone else had ever run. We'd discussed the possibility of running from the front, but considered that there was a far greater chance in an Olympic final, where anyone can be inspired on the day to do something far beyond their previous form, to do all the work for just such a runner and then get stuffed on the run-in. Not that we considered it *would* happen, and certainly the temptation was there. I could probably have got away with it, keeping clear of the bargeing and spiking, avoiding being boxed or forced to run wide. But ultimately we decided, on the assumption of my having the fastest basic speed, that the safest race was still to hold back, sit in on the pace of the leaders, cover anything that happened up front, and kick somewhere round the last bend. We knew I had the speed over 150 metres for it not to be a risk, and the faster the early race, the more I should have in hand, relative to the others, in the final stages. ❢

The semi-final times had been nothing special, and Seb would start the final even more a favourite than Juantorena in Montreal. The draw the night before had placed him in the outside lane of the eight runners, giving him all the options, and none of the dangers of having opponents cut across him in the sprint for the second bend after the lane-break following the first bend. I still believed he should run from the front, but it was none of my business, and I respected his and Peter's judgement enough to prevent me throwing in gratuitous doubts from my position of a privileged bystander. The draw for the final, with qualifying times and personal bests prior to the Games, was:

	Qualifying time	Personal best
Nikolai Kirov (USSR)	1:46·6	1:45·6
Steve Ovett (GB)	1:46·6	1:44·1
Alberto Guimaraes (BRAZIL)	1:46·9	1:46·0
Detlef Wagenknecht (GDR)	1:46·7	1:45·9
Dave Warren (GB)	1:47·2	1:46·2
Jose Marajo (France)	1:47·3	1:43·9
Andreas Busse (GDR)	1:46·9	1:44·8
Sebastian Coe (GB)	1:46·7	1:42·4

Peter without actually being worried, considered that the main threat – Ovett apart – would come from Wagenknecht, and he felt that Marajo, qualifying as a fastest loser, had not shown the sort of form to approach his personal best of 1:43·9. In his heart he knew, and Seb knew, that providing he gave himself the chance, by positioning himself in the right place at the right time, short of injury there could only be one winner. But what was to be the worst day of Seb's young life began badly.

        ❝ I've never known pressure like it. I thought people had exaggerated, but they hadn't. There was no comparison. I'd felt pressure going into the Europa Cup final the year before, but it just wasn't the same thing. It began after the semi-final. I can remember looking down into my food at dinner amid the hubbub of the huge crowded restaurant, and glancing up and catching Peter's eye. He must have sensed I was uneasy because he smiled and said, 'don't start *now*'. It was unusual for me, I'd never been like that so long before a race. I had the worst night's sleep I've ever had, just lying there listening to my own heartbeat, thinking to myself, you've coped with the pressure all year, for heaven's sake take a grip! But it was the same next day. At lunch I knocked over my orange juice, and then dropped the cream carton into my cup of coffee. I suddenly felt ungainly, conscious of my own awkwardness. That morning I'd seen Kenny Mays of the *Daily*

Telegraph, and he'd said with that friendly leer of his, 'well, 7.30 tonight, the moment I've been waiting for'. The moment *he* had been waiting for! It was just the kind of well-meant comment that tightens your nerves another turn. In the afternoon I couldn't sleep again, which is rare for me. Peter was up in the room, and he knew what was going on, but he knew that saying anything wouldn't help.

I can remember the relief of getting on the move at last, going down to the stadium. But leaving the Village my attitude was all wrong. I wanted to hurry into the warm up, I didn't want to be alone. I'd already gone through the nervous bit, and now I was detached, disconnected. Mentally, I was an hour ahead of schedule. Normally, the detached phase happens in the few minutes before the race, when you've done the physical and mental wind-up and you're ready to cut out everything: voices, faces, sounds. But I was like this with forty-five minutes still to go. The race had that written all over it, it was a disinterested race, someone going through the motions. After the warm up there was the long walk over the bridge to the main stadium. Steve had looked tense. He and Harry were together, ahead of Peter and me, with the British team managers at the back. They wished us good luck, and we went down into the little preparation room where we got our lane numbers for our shorts, and they checked the number and length of our spikes. **❯**

As Peter watched Seb disappear into the bowels of the stadium he was aware that all was not well with his athlete, as he had been for some time. His problem was that he was not really sure *what* was wrong, nor how best to correct it. Many weeks later, turning the race over in his mind for the hundredth time, he would admit to me:

'I have to ask myself why, of all times, did I not prepare him properly – *if* I didn't? I had always said that if he lost it would be my fault. That's why, afterwards, I was ashamed. For myself. I had sensed for a while before the final that he was detached, almost inert, but I was alert to the danger of putting *more* pressure on him. He doesn't like me to bother him in the hour before a big race. Our work together has by then been done, and he's locked into himself in mental preparation. In

that last hour I'm just a valet. My suggesting he might be about
to lose was the last thing he needed. I couldn't think what I
should do, but getting it wrong could have been even worse
than doing nothing. My fear was to undermine him, even
knowing he was not properly switched on. The point was that
at 800 metres he had to be *so* bad to lose, I couldn't conceive
that, even though he was a shade sluggish, he would blow it. I
must have supposed subconsciously that he would still be OK.
I knew he was, at his best, immeasurably better than anyone
else in the race. It was nonsense to suggest, as David Coleman
did in the Sportsview Personality of the Year programme, that
Seb was tactically naïve. He had proved himself in some hard
races, without me. What I didn't know at that moment before
the 800 metres was how to say something to sharpen him without creating doubt. I could imagine him looking at me and
saying, "Christ, what a thing to say to me at this moment!"
So I said nothing.'

The relationship between a great athlete and his coach, however
stable in times of calm, can be as volatile as a love affair when
under pressure.

❖ I'd changed my official-issue vest because the seams
had been chafing, and had had my race number, 254 – the same
throughout the Games – restitched onto the old GB shirt in which
I had broken the world records. Over at the warm up track the two
East Germans had been striding together, so had Steve and Dave,
and it vaguely crossed my mind that they might have planned
something together. But then I realized that on balance this was
silly; I couldn't believe that anyone would go into an Olympic
final and sacrifice his own chance for someone else. Besides, I
consoled myself, it was not now in Steve's interest to have a fast
early pace. I was beginning to be a little more keyed up, but I still
wasn't mentally right. The wretched business of being made to
walk everywhere in single file in lane order irked me, and I took a
delight now, and again in the 1,500 metres final, in breaking rank.
We filed out past the window of the kitchens under the stadium,
and I was acutely aware of the rancid, sickly smell. We put our
gear in the plastic baskets; I could hear the names being called out
over the loud-speakers. We were allowed a brief warm up on the

97

track, had to go back into the tunnel afterwards, then out again once more in lane order to the start. Going to the line I can only remember feeling utterly empty. For me the race would be memorable only for the little I could remember about it afterwards. As we waited in the tunnel, Steve had said to me: 'It's stupid to think we're doing this here for nothing, when we could turn professional and fill a stadium on our own.' **?**

It was cooler than it had been in the past few days, and the flags around the rim of the stadium were stiffening in a strong wind which did not penetrate down as far as the runners. Already the floodlights were on in the half light of the evening. As the runners went to the line Sara Simeone, who had obliged Seb to dodge round her during the warm up, dislodged the bar in the women's high jump. The moment the gun went, Seb moved off as if it was the start of a 10,000 metres race. I couldn't believe it. He looked as if he was running in soft sand. At the lane break, it was Guimaraes of Brazil leading from Kirov, and as they approached the second bend Ovett was badly boxed as the runners converged in front of him, coming across from the outside, while he attempted to hold his ground in the second lane where he had begun. Coming off the first bend, Seb had made no attempt to accelerate and close on the leaders; in the next few seconds that seemed no bad thing.

❝ I remember the gun going and feeling sluggish, running without conviction. There was so much that was adrift. I came off the lane break after 130 metres with no awareness of anyone's positions. I was thinking of *nothing*! Going into the second bend I was probably in my best position in the race, fifth or sixth, with Ovett just in front of me. **?**

It was now that Ovett vigorously handed off Wagenknecht. The 6 foot 4 inch East German lost his balance and, in attempting to stay on his feet, veered outwards and, in turn, impeded Marajo, who almost went down. A few strides further on, Ovett swerved to the right, and again Marajo was impeded. Coming into the home straight for the first time, Guimaraes was still in the lead but with the entire field still bunched together within three strides, Seb loping along on the outside at the back, with Ovett caught with a wall of runners in front of him. Approaching the bell, Ovett tried to force his way between Wagenknecht and Kirov -- and failed. As Guimaraes went through the half way in 54·5, Ovett was sixth, and Seb last.

6 Running wide off the second bend, and wide down the straight, I was conscious of being last at the bell but I still had a total lack of urgency, perhaps because the field was so bunched. What I had no awareness of was how hopelessly compromised Steve was at that stage. When I saw the video I realized it was one of the several opportunities I had to make a decisive move. Instead, I continued to run wide round the third bend. 9

Here Warren made a burst to the front past the Brazilian; Kirov following, with Ovett accelerating out of the bend to keep in touch. Still Seb failed to react. Going into the final bend Kirov went past Warren and, with 200 metres to go, led Ovett by a couple of strides, with Guimaraes and Wagenknecht another two strides down on Ovett, and Coe, Busse, and Marajo together another three metres down.

6 Down the back straight I still felt, erroneously, that I was OK; I was aware that Kirov had surged, but until we turned into the bend I wasn't aware how much, because of the runners in between. Into the final bend I still hadn't been buried, but I hung back as Busse and Marajo went by. 9

It was allowing himself to be boxed at this moment which finally cost Seb the race. By the time he changed gear and moved outside the others, he was some twelve to thirteen metres, or about six strides, adrift of the leader. Coming off the final bend Ovett made his move and overtook Kirov. Way back, Seb was at last responding. Knowing in my heart it was a vain hope even for Seb, I turned to Ian Wooldridge of the *Daily Mail*, high up in the press box, and said, 'here he comes!' Seb ripped past Busse and

Marajo, then the fading Wagenknecht and Guimaraes. With forty metres to go he was third and still gaining on Kirov and Ovett. With twenty metres to go he passed Kirov, and now his astonishing sprint was spent and in the last few strides he could close no further on Ovett. By a substantial three metres the gold medal was Ovett's in 1:45·4.

‘When Steve made his move off the final bend he was about five strides up, and by the time I reacted to get clear of Busse and Marajo, Steve must have been eight strides up. That's fifteen metres. Entering the final straight, I knew that I'd probably blown it, that it was going to mean a fantastic effort to pull back. Suddenly I was going past people. One went, and I was fifth; two more, and I was third and overhauling Kirov. I wondered if I was even going to get a medal. I didn't know how well I'd run the last 150 metres until I came into the press conference half an hour later and you, David, said, 'like a train', and I thought 'Oh God!' I'd grown accustomed to taking liberties in one or two races in the previous year, to running wide from the back, and now, in the most devastating way, I'd discovered you can't do that in an Olympic final. I wasted so much nervous energy before the race, I'd never been as nervous before, yet look at the chances the race still gave me! Going into the final bend I thought I was in contention, then suddenly realized it was a hell of a gap and that I was going to have to run myself out even to get a medal.

With thirty metres to go I knew I was not going to win. At the finish I just went off the track and the extraordinary thing was that my first reaction was a huge feeling of relief rather than disappointment. That it was *over*. I went into the doping test room still uninterested. Sara Simeone was there, crying, having just won her gold. I was reacting in the same way as people often do after a car accident, wanting only to get away from the scene. Steve was coughing and looked fatigued. I was in and out of the dope test in minutes . . . and I'd lost. It told me just how much I'd failed to use my strength on the track.

As we came out for the medal ceremony it was at last beginning to sink in, the size of the disaster. There was the incessant clicking of cameras: will you and Steve shake hands, will you shake your fist over his head, will you . . . will you . . . Up on the rostrum I *did* shake Steve's hand. Clive James in *The Observer* wrote that I looked as if I'd just been handed a turd, which was a bit harsh; I don't think I was discourteous to Steve. I was just blank, I didn't hear the Olympic hymn as the Olympic flags were raised, or notice the re-run of the finish on the giant electronic screen. At the time, and since the Games, a few people have said that I looked grim and seemed less than generous in defeat. But it had nothing to do with losing to Steve, I was just totally disconnected, I knew I had run appallingly in what was supposed to be *my* event, and the numbness would have been the same whoever had won. That rostrum was no place to be smiling after tossing the race away.

Back in the tunnel I was sitting in a chair with my head in my hands. Mike Murphy of BBC TV came up to me in a friendly way, and with that aggressive forefinger push of his glasses on the bridge of his nose, said, 'get your f------ head up, Coe'. He meant well, knowing I had to pull myself together for the 1,500 metres. But both the press and TV had wanted me to win because of Steve's refusal to co-operate with them, they wanted it as much for themselves as for me, I suspected. If I'd lost to Walker or Bayi or Scott, the media wouldn't have put the same pressure on me as they did now. It was an added burden I didn't need. **9**

Up in the press and commentary boxes, many were waiting for a protest by either the East Germans or the French. Whether or not it might have been upheld, it never came. Twice, at 200 metres and again at 450 metres, Ovett had, in the words of Cliff Temple in *The Sunday Times*, 'almost literally fought his way out of trouble'. Chris Brasher said in *The Observer*, 'it was perilously close to the rules', while the authoritative *Athletics Weekly*'s Mel Watman claimed: 'Ovett ran so physical a race that he can consider himself lucky not to have been disqualified.' Ovett himself would admit in an interview for ITV with Metcalfe: 'If anyone was guilty of doing more than their fair share of pushing, it was probably me. I can be called the worst of the bunch, but I honestly believe that everyone ran a fair race. People were wearing half-inch spikes, and if anyone gets close to you, you fend them off because they are dangerous. It looks as if you're pushing, but it's safety precautions.' Henry Cooper, giving his considered view on television, said in his inimitable cockney vernacular: 'The difference was between one geeser 'oo knew 'ow to use 'is elbows, and one 'oo didn't. Blimey, I thought athletics was a gen'lman's sport!' Neil Amdur, a droll New Yorker who knows the athletics scene intimately, said as we filed down to the interview room in Moscow: 'It was a race without history.'

❝ Only after I'd seen the video did I realize how physical Steve had been. I felt it had contributed to the tattiness of the race. It lowered the standing of athletics. I was very surprised the East Germans and French didn't make more of it. I would hate to think that as a result of that final we might breed a race of middle-distance runners who breast-stroke their way out of a scrum. The 800 metres is unique, because nowadays it is almost a sprint the whole way, just not in lanes for the last 670 metres. It's eight guys fighting for position in a sprint spread over two-and-a-half lanes. Of course you have to react tactically, and I didn't. But if you accept the development of physical contact, then tactics mean nothing, and the roughest man is going to win. You cannot equate racing ability with handing people off, as some of the press did. It is tactically allowable to protect the space you have earned by your pace or your positioning, but *not* to gain space that is occupied by somebody else which you would prefer. That is not tactical intelligence, it's the negation of it. ❞

Ovett, as in Prague, declined to attend the official press conference. When Seb arrived, more with the air of an eight-year-old who has just been pulled out of the canal than an Olympic silver medallist, Peter was already sitting there at the table alongside the Master of Ceremonies. By facing up to the world's press after such a personal howler, Seb was showing considerably more nerve than he had in the race. As he took his seat Peter, who had not yet spoken to him, whispered in his ear, 'you ran like an idiot', though his face contained not a trace of criticism. Still in a daze, Seb answered the battery of questions: yes, I made tactical errors; no, I didn't respond at the right moments; my intention was to do nothing more than anyone else did at the front and to cover the breaks, but I didn't; obviously there was a lot of pressure but at this level you have to expect it . . .

❝ It was like an autopsy in there. Malcolm Brammer from Sheffield was near to tears, Neil Allen looked awful. Colin Hart's (athletics correspondent of *The Sun*) face suggested he'd lost a pile. Peter was very good, he didn't need to tell me how badly I'd run. I knew all too well, and I knew how hard I'd hit him. ❞

Father and son battled their way through the crush of reporters and down the steps of the stadium to look for their official car back to the Village. Outside it was dark. Peter put his arm round Seb, Malcolm was on the other side of him. I muttered to Peter, 'quickly, there's a camera unit after him', as a hand-held camera and sound man tried to get round in front of them. Seb was shaking, close to tears: they were tears of anger more than disappointment. Behind us, looming out of the darkness, padded Jim Lawton, a former *Express* colleague now working in Vancouver. Jim, always a sensitive writer, had seen all he needed to know from some yards off, and discreetly turned back towards the press room.

We found the car, after first going to the wrong warm-up track. As we crossed the bridge for the second time, Seb asked bitterly, 'how much did I make up?' I said ten metres. 'Oh, Christ', he said again as the magnitude of his error sank deeper into his at last conscious brain. We bundled into the car and the impassive Russian chauffeur moved off. In his mis-adjusted driving mirror I could see Peter in the back seat with his arm around Seb, the way you comfort your infant child when it comes to your bed in the middle of the night troubled by a nightmare. There was no recrimination there, only mutual love and shared grief. It was not a time for talk, and I stared ahead through the windscreen at the wide, now almost deserted road back to the Village. On arrival I had to enter by a different gate. In case I failed to gain admission to join them for dinner, Seb said, 'thanks for caring', and I said, 'it's disproved nothing, winning the 1,500 metres can now only be even sweeter'.

❝ I was grateful for the darkness. I kept thinking why now, why the Olympics, why not Cudworth, or Hull? I just hadn't believed it could happen to me, and now suddenly there was this nagging fear: is this, like Prague, going to be the story of my career, missing out when it really matters? Back in our block, Mary Peters threw her arms round me in tears. I had a shower and went to bed. A few came to the room, Brendan was the first. 'You just didn't race, did you, you froze.' I felt so stupid, that others could remember so much about the race and I could remember almost nothing. **)**

I had caught the last bus from the Village back to the centre of Moscow shortly before midnight. I knew that the loneliest woman in Britain at this moment was probably Angela. I took a cab from the press centre back to the Rossiya, and called her on the direct dial telephone from my room, which occasionally worked first time, or could take up to thirty attempts to get through to London depending, I suppose, on what sort of mood eavesdropping Boris was in. Tonight I was lucky. Angela answered: surprised, alarmed. In the past, she had told me previously, she had been dismayed at the apparent ruthlessness of the schedules which her husband had set her son, thinking 'it shouldn't happen to a dog'. She herself came from the sort of background in which you apologized for winning at tennis, but slowly she had become accustomed to the evident streak of aggression in her otherwise shy son. Her first worry now was not that he had lost, but what effect defeat might have had upon him. She longed to be near him, to tell him it was only a *race*. To me she said anxiously: 'How is he, how has he taken it, do you think he'll retire if he doesn't win the 1,500 metres?'. 'No,' I said, 'I don't think he'll retire, he's angry as much as disappointed. Give him a day or two and he'll have recovered. I'm doubling all my bets on the 1,500 metres.'

On the sixth floor of the British quarters, son and father hardly slept, talking the night away in a subdued, at times agonized, at times rational, post mortem. People are apt to say, glibly, that they would give their right arm for something, but when the father now said he would give his for his son's success in the 1,500 metres, I would accept that he truly meant it.

7: Dark Days

❬ The next morning when I got up, Daley came bouncing in, full of life as ever. 'What's the weather like?' he asked. 'Looks a bit silver to me', I said. 'I've been thinking,' Daley mused, at his most mischievous, 'after you've won the 1,500 metres, why don't we get a picture of Mrs Ovett with his medal, your Dad with yours, and my Auntie Doreen with mine. The press would just love that!' I laughed, but I didn't feel like laughing. The worst hangover imaginable could not compare with what I felt when I woke up. To rub it in, the celebrations for Allan Wells' gold in the 100 metres had still been going on in the room next door – telegrams arriving, a continuous noise, just as it should have been, but it made it twice as bad for me.

Had winning bred complacency in me? I had possibly felt deep down that the 800 metres would come *to* me, I probably didn't give it enough thought. What I needed now was a good long run to clear my mind and my body, so I left the Village to do ten or eleven miles on the road in under the hour. I was tracked the *whole* way by a carload of British photographers. I know that up to a point it's their job, but I felt they were like vultures. That's irrational, because you like the attention when you've won, when they capture a happy face or a good run. But that morning I felt it was an intrusion. I found out later that one of the tabloid papers had carried a picture the next morning under the headline 'Trail of Shame'. Fortunately I didn't know about it at the time. I just felt better for the run, resolutely ignoring the unwelcome dawn patrol. ❭

The papers back home were fierce in their dismissal of Seb as just one more in the long line of line-breakers who allegedly did not possess the innate racing brain when it came to a major championship final. Peter Hildreth in the *Sunday Telegraph* went even farther, and suggested that Seb had an inherent lack of physical strength for the occasion, saying:

'No power on earth can now prevent Ovett from winning the 1,500 metres on Friday. That is, after all, his priority and Coe's weaker distance. Any chance of Coe beating Ovett in the 1,500 metres would have had to follow his establishing a moral ascendancy in the 800 metres which he singularly failed to do. As the pair have not met since two years ago, when Ovett beat Coe for the silver medal in the European Championship, there has been little chance to make a direct comparison. While I do not suggest that either of these outstanding runners takes anabolic steroids or any other drugs, the palpable contrast between them in general physical profile and musculature is an object lesson.'

John Rodda of *The Guardian,* who has seen more athletics than most and, in collaboration with Lord Killanin, was the author of a history of the Olympics, was dismissive of both Seb and the race itself:

'The first instalment of the Coe v Ovett saga was a bad ticket-seller for the next . . . Ovett won and why he did not wave an arm down the finishing straight I do not know, unless it is that he has some respect for the dignity of even these Olympic Games. In the event he won the race as though he were on the athletic circus somewhere, turning out a performance against a gathering of well-meaning locals. It was a flat, anti-climactic affair that was all over as soon as Ovett raised the pace around the last bend. It was a race about a loser rather than a winner. Coe has much to do in the 1,500 metres to reject the accusation that he is not a man who can cope with championship racing. His frail frame can be prepared for that one explosive night in Oslo or Zürich, where he can run the world off its feet, but in the demanding cockpit of a championship he is left wanting both mentally and physically, on this evidence. The last time he came on this parade was in the European Championships two years ago, and there he followed home Ovett when both were beaten. Since then he has not much bothered with championships, even domestic ones, and his studied avoidance of Ovett . . . has now come home to roost. It was never less than a well thought out way of running, but the more simplistic idea of

106

putting his toe in the bath to see how hot the water is would have proved a better scheme. The red carpet for victory was rolled out on Saturday and he did not see it. Coe, from the outside lane, had the opportunity, and took it, to avoid the bumping by running wide. No one wanted to do the front work and the elbows were clashing when the digital clock clicked up a first lap of 54·3. Ovett was locked in a box with Wagenknecht banging him in the ribs. It was the moment for Coe to fly; he would, with his acceleration, have been thirty metres clear before Ovett could have escaped and that would have been enough.'

Watman, in spite of his reservations about Ovett's rough tactics, asserted in *Athletics Weekly:* 'One can state with some authority that Steve is the greatest big-time competitor ever to wear the British vest.' And in the *Express* I wrote:

'Ovett crushingly taught Coe the age old Olympic lesson in Saturday's long awaited 800 metres final – first is first, second is nowhere. The experienced, gritty racer beat the finely tuned record-breaker in a slow affair which was an anti-climax. Now a huge question mark hangs over Coe. Unless he exacts revenge in Friday's 1,500 metres final, or at least pushes Ovett to a new world record, his prestige will take a hammering. While Ovett is poised to emulate New Zealander Peter Snell's 1964 double in Tokyo, Coe has first to recover from his novice-like defeat.'

From the evidence, I was sure he could.

❜ It was natural for people to ask themselves, 'has the guy got brains?' In fact, I wasn't aware of the extent of the criticism because I deliberately hadn't read a single newspaper all the time I was in the Village. But I did sit down and wonder whether it was a one-off blunder, whether I did have the racing intelligence. I mentioned to Peter that maybe in future I should find a few more races where there was some messing about in the early stages. How can a silver medal mean nothing? At the kind of level Steve and I had lived at, the life-style we'd adopted, you don't regard a silver medal as acceptable. You don't totally reorganize your life for a year, relinquishing friends and normal contacts, with a view to winning the silver. Even Steve admitted to me, 'I don't know sometimes if it's worth it'. Eamonn Coghlan knew how I felt, he told me, 'I was the fastest finisher in the 1,500 metres in Montreal and threw it away, there was a wall in front and I was boxed, I should have had a medal.' I'm willing to accept, in retrospect, that the magnitude of the Games may have got to me, the pressure did undermine me. **)**

The pressure did not lessen, it intensified. Not only did Seb realize that his reputation with the public and his status within athletics depended upon a convincing display on Friday, but he had become aware of a planned TV coup which would centre upon Ovett if he now achieved the double. There was a move, according to reliable sources, to promote a series of world-wide invitation meetings packaged around Ovett. If Seb lost, it was probable that he would be frozen out of the series, which would be designed to launch Ovett to a new clutch of world records. Ovett had already claimed in a Sunday newspaper, the day after his gold medal in the 800 metres, that he and Seb were 'worth millions in promotional terms'. But Seb was against both a professional circus, and also the concept of a TV spectacular staged under existing 'amateur' regulations . . . without him! The only way to torpedo the plan was to win the 1,500 metres.

He was also now put under additional pressure, inadvertently, by Peter. From the experience of his ten-mile morning run, Seb sensed that it would be best to keep out of the way of the press for a while. But Peter, passing the time mid-morning as usual at the open-air café of the international area of the Village, gave an interview to the daily paper correspondents, which was published on the Monday. In it he repeated, being the direct man he is, the opinion he had expressed to Seb: that he had 'run like an idiot'. He also talked of humiliation.

Words such as 'idiot' and 'humiliation' are the twenty pound notes of journalistic currency. The reporter confronted by them in an interview would be failing in his trade if he did not use them in the controversial circumstances of such an Olympic upset. It is not the job of the writer to protect the speaker from his own indiscretions. Many reporters, already disposed to be critical of either the runner or his coach or both after such a gaffe, now also discovered, as they thought, the coach putting the boot in about his son. Theirs was not to reason why. Peter's words were splashed liberally over Monday's breakfast tables.

By Tuesday lunchtime the impact at home of father slamming son had been beamed back to the Village. Seb confronted Peter in something of a quandary. He was annoyed at his father's indiscretion, yet still carried a sense of guilt that he *had* badly let down the man who had given him such devotion, emotional and practical. Peter explained his actions, saying: 'Under no circumstances was I going to let the press think it was the *real* you out there. It wasn't bad luck, you weren't beaten, you *lost* it. The more people who realized that the better.'

❛ I wouldn't have minded if Peter had said it was humiliating for *him*. It was. People were entitled to ask what kind of advice he'd been giving me, but on balance I was less annoyed with Peter's public comments than about some of the press comment on him. To have Hugh McIlvanney of *The Observer* say that Peter 'shadowed me everywhere' I found insulting. If I'd known at the time, instead of when I got back to England, I'd have been furious. What right had he to make such assumptions about my father, how much had he really seen us working together? For a long time I had put up with the uninformed comment that Peter's coaching was something to boost his own ego. Enormously strong ties are developed between athlete and coach, and people were entitled to criticize my running, or Peter's coaching, but *not* our relationship after only the most casual observation.

It was an embarrassing few days with the press whenever I met any of them in the Village. Many of them were avoiding my eye because *they* were embarrassed. They'd say, 'well, there's still Friday, you can do it', but their manner and their eyes told me they didn't believe it. Not that I hold that against any of them, why should they have thought otherwise? Colin Hart saw me and said good humouredly, 'I'm not going to say anything, but you'd better bloody well do it next time!' And Benny Hill of the *Sheffield Morning Telegraph* said to me when I got home, 'you set them all up, what else could they write?' But it did get under my skin a bit, that so many of the press were emphatic that I wasn't a racer, that they seemed to overlook the way I won the

Europa Cup, that they wouldn't allow me that one horrible mistake. I suppose it was the fact that it came on top of Prague.

Yet from the moment I had that run on Sunday morning I felt I was on the path to recovery. I had lunch and went down to the stadium to watch the final of the 10,000 metres. The photographers seemed as intent on me as on the race, constantly turning to point their telescopic 'missile launchers' at me in the stand. It was a great race, Yifter winning after such a brave bid by Viren, and it did me good to get back to the atmosphere of the track. Perhaps I'd isolated myself too much before the 800 metres. When I came out from the stadium I met Ron Pickering from BBC TV, who said, 'people are wondering if we've got any friends left'. Steve had just given his exclusive interview with Metcalfe for ITV, and this had left the BBC standing at the post a bit. I agreed to do an interview for them with Harry Carpenter, but it made me feel that I was having to carry not only myself, but people in the media. One got the impression that the competition between the two channels was as important as the Games! 〉

On Tuesday, the day before the 1,500 metres heats, Seb received a letter from Chris Brasher in which he had outlined opinions on how Seb should win the 1,500 metres, following discussions he had had with Australian former multi world-record holder Ron Clarke. The sentiments of Brasher and Clarke were admirable: the race plan they had devised for Seb less certain. Brasher wrote:

'Your own talent has given you the chance to emerge as *the* champion of these games. As Ron says, you have to take your chance when it is there, and he missed his in the 5,000 metres in Tokyo. No pace can drop you off, and you are also the fastest in the field, and that is an unbeatable combination. The only person who can beat you is yourself. Because you cannot be dropped and you are also the fastest, you are the Hunter. You can dictate the race. Ron thinks you are still the best, but now a lot of people think the other bloke is. All it needs is an iron determination in your heart. Get that into your mind. And then, in the race, relax, move up, and strike.'

In between this fundamental and encouraging advice were elaborate instructions on the tactics which Seb should employ against either Bayi or Ovett or both. While the encouragement was the sincere contribution of two former world-class runners to another, the tactical recommendations rather presumed an absence of discussions between Seb and his father!

‘ It was kind of Chris to take the trouble, and I was grateful for the gesture, for the knowledge that two men such as they should consider I was unbeatable if I ran it the right way – though their way was not quite the same as mine, and in the event Bayi withdrew to concentrate on the 3,000 metres steeplechase. He was determined to win Tanzania's first ever medal in the Games, he wanted that more than any personal glory and in the end he got the silver, after a dramatic race in which he led by almost fifty metres with three laps to go and was finally caught by Malinowski, that marvellously talented Pole who was so sadly killed a year later. It was on the Tuesday, the same day as I received Brasher's letter, that Brendan started his psychotherapy, threatening me with the idea that if I lost again there would be only one runner in Britain who mattered, that if I lost again the critics would be bracketing me with Dave Bedford, a record breaker who had flopped in the Munich Olympics and the Christchurch Commonwealth Games. ‘Do you want that?’

I felt I was now getting back into a state of aggression, partly through anger at my own performance, partly because everyone was writing me off so quickly. It would be all very well for David Coleman to say after the 1,500 metres ‘you don't become a bad athlete overnight’, but that hadn't always been his view during the previous week. The Wednesday of the first round of the 1,500 metres was the hottest day of the Games yet, but the heats on the whole were unexceptional. In mine, I went to the front and stayed there, and ran down the final straight together with Fontanella of Italy, with him looking sideways at me most of the way. After the race I went back into the stadium to watch the rest of the day with Peter. He was slightly annoyed that I'd not won, Fontanella had got the verdict by inches in the identical time of 3:40·1. Peter had said, ‘go out and run like a world record holder and cleanse yourself’. He was beginning to be quite severe with me. We went back to the Village and had a large meal, cooked meat, potatoes, sweet-corn, and two pints of orange juice – the middle distance runner's diet. Then a massage back in the British quarters, and bed. 〝

With the first four in each heat and the two fastest losers to qualify for the semi-finals, Steve Cram had to work hard at the finish in the first heat, won by Marajo, to get in front of the Russian Yakoylev for the fourth place. Ovett took the fourth heat a stride ahead of Jurgen Straub of East Germany in 3:36·8. The draw for the two semis kept Ovett and Coe apart, and Ovett seemed to me to have the harder prospect. His draw included Malozemlin, the fancied Russian, Busse, Cram, Zdravkovic, and Loikanen of Finland. Seb's only serious challenger was Straub. In the event it was Seb who had to run the faster to be first home – after a considerable scare before the race.

〝 I had a good ten hours' sleep after the heats, and had two miles of easy jogging early in the morning. I somehow felt it would be the hardest of the two semi-finals, and I was pleased it was going to be late in the evening, after nine, which is when I'm at my best. I wanted to win well, a full dress rehearsal for the following day. I was walking back to the Village after lunch when suddenly I had stomach pains. I'd got the bug which had K.O.'d Dave Moorcroft! I immediately took tablets from the team doctor to close me up, thinking, 'this is all I need!' I didn't panic, I went to bed and slept. The tablets worked, sealed me up, but I felt uncomfortable inside, carrying all that rubbish.

Apart from needing physiotherapy to keep my hamstring flexible, my muscular state was improving all the time. I travelled down to the stadium for the semis with Steve and Harry, we had a car booked and offered them and Steve Cram a lift and arranged a time to collect them afterwards, but when it came they didn't turn up. I was in the second race, and the tone was set in the first few strides when Tischenko, the Russian, cut across from the outside. I remember handing him off and moving to the front, in behind Straub, who led for the first two laps. Down the back straight for the third time I surged to keep pace with Nemeth of Austria as he came through, and I handed off Straub as he tried to come with us. At the bell I was just behind Nemeth, followed by Straub and Marajo. On the last bend I stupidly allowed Fontanella and Marajo to go past me on the outside, temporarily boxing me in, and I had to produce a really fierce burst to get clear again. I was aware I had made a mistake, but not how glaring it was till I caught Peter's eye after the race. His expression said, 'what are you trying to do to me?' For three days he'd been drumming into me: 'Be in touch with the leader, no more than a stride down going into the last bend, and run wide almost into the second lane, so that if anybody tries to go past they have to run really wide, and you still have the space to respond and go past the leader if you need to.' 〉

Up in the stand Brasher and Clarke looked at each other and agreed: 'He's had it. He hasn't got a tactical brain.' It had certainly been a blunder, but the acceleration with which Seb corrected it was one of the most electric of any race in the Games. He crossed the line a fraction ahead of Straub in 3:39·4, almost four seconds faster than Ovett's winning time in the first semi. Cram, in a desperate finish with Malozemlin in which both were given the same time of 3:43·6, had just squeezed fourth place to qualify for the final at the age of nineteen. Plachy of Czechoslovakia, fifth in Coe's semi, was the fastest 'loser' to make up the nine in the final. They would be:

	Qualifying time	Personal best
Jurgen Straub (GDR)	3:39·4	3:33·7
Jose Marajo (France)	3:39·6	3:35·1
Andreas Busse (GDR)	3:43·5	3:37·1
Steve Cram (GB)	3:43·6	3:35·6
Vittorio Fontanella (Italy)	3:40·1	3:38·3
Sebastian Coe (GB)	3:39·4	3:32·1
Jozef Plachy (Czechoslovakia)	3:40·4	3:37·2
Steve Ovett (GB)	3:43·1	3:32·1
Dragan Zdravkovic (Yugoslavia)	3:43·4	3:38·0

〈 I suppose you could say my 1,500 metres semi-final wasn't any better than the 800 metres final as a bargeing match. I felt ashamed about it, even more so when people came up afterwards and said, 'that's the way, we knew you were on the way back when you started throwing them out of your path!' I had to play down being boxed in, especially when I saw Peter's face. As we sat by the warm-up track afterwards Peter was saying, 'if you do that tomorrow, you're dead'. I did six or seven laps to warm down in the dark, I didn't want to leave the junk in my legs from a fairly fast race. It was late before we had dinner and I finally got to bed. But I slept very well. Instead of the nerves I had before the 800 metres, I was now excited by the final of the 1,500 metres, I wanted to get out there and enjoy it. **)**

Peter and I leaned on the railing of the warm-up track as Seb floated round, disappearing into the darkness on the far side and then reappearing into the finishing straight, illuminated dimly by a few bulbs along the front of the small changing pavilion. Two other shadowy figures were warming down: Seb's German rivals Straub and Busse, observed by a posse of coaches. Peter looked tired and drawn. He had been troubled by a bad ankle, from the miles of walking one had to do around the Village and the stadium and the hotels. He was sixty, and the pressure was getting at him, too. The tension was if anything worse for him than for his son because, as with any coach, once any race began, he was powerless to affect the outcome. As we stared out now into the darkness, he was no longer planning, just day-dreaming about what he knew was possible but at that moment was still far off. 'At least his stomach held out', he said to me without turning his head, knowing that Seb's stomach was the least of the problems. The weak electric light accentuated the lines in Peter's thin face; like his son he'd come a long way, at a time of life when the effort was going to show. He said: 'If he only does what he's capable of, there is no one tomorrow who will touch him. Not just because it's painful, but I'd give my right arm for him to go the line again tomorrow in the same frame of mind as he did for the Oslo Mile last year. *That* was my runner.' Seb came off the track smiling and relaxed. Maybe he would go to the line 'all together'.

Brasher and Clark were not alone, even if in a minority, in believing that the gun would go with Seb the logical favourite. Cliff Temple had written after the 800 metres final: 'Last night's results may have only a marginal effect on the 1,500 metres. The demands are slightly different: four years ago John Walker of

New Zealand was eliminated in his 800 metres heat but he still went on to win the 1,500 metres final. Friday's race is still the big showdown.' After the evening's two semi-finals I had cabled to the *Express:* 'If Sebastian Coe is within striking distance of Steve Ovett 200 metres from the finish of today's classic Olympic 1,500 metres final, he will win.'

In all his races thus far Ovett had been sign-writing in the air with his right hand after he crossed the line: a message, which was said to be I.L.Y. for 'I Love You', aimed at the television cameras for the benefit of his girlfriend back home. As this supreme runner had entered the final straight of his semi-final, he had waved cheerily to his mother in the crowd. I sensed he was taunting destiny.

8: Release

Early on the day of the final, under yet another cloudless blue sky, I made the ten mile journey out to the Village and there, on a grassy bank, I found Kenny Moore, US marathon runner and writer for *Sports Illustrated,* looking rather forlorn in singlet and tracksuit bottom and his inevitable training shoes. 'Every time I ring my office and talk to them, they say "fine, Kenny, but you've only got half of the story". They're convinced Ovett is going to win again, it's *the* event of the whole Games back in the States, and I need to get hold of Steve, but I can never find the fellow.' Kenny, a personal friend of the Coes, had the look of a man who has an important plane to catch and is convinced he is going to miss it. Was even he now doubting Seb, I thought to myself? His doubt would have been magnified had he known the extent of the trouble from Seb's sciatic-related hamstring.

❝ It was vital that I was able to get a really good massage twice a day. Helen Bristow, the physio who looked after me, did an exceptional job, she worked very hard to keep the tendon loose. It showed her integrity, too, she never spoke a word to anyone, not even to her several friends among the press, whom she had known for a number of years. The news would have aroused the press enormously; but if I'd let it be known at the time and then lost again, it would have been said it was sour grapes. The work of all the physios, who were on duty from dawn till midnight and hardly ever had the chance even to leave the Village, could not have been more selfless and painstaking. They gave us psychotherapy as much as physiotherapy. Allan Wells was convinced at one stage that he had torn muscle fibres, when in fact he'd only had cramp in the middle of the night. They cured him and calmed him down.

Everyone out there on the administrative side did a marvellous job, too. The team managers Nick Whitehead, Lynn Davies, and

Mary Peters didn't miss a trick. It was a colossal improvement on the old days, having people who were *for* the athletes and not for themselves. They were working an eighteen-hour day, right down to getting the draws off the computer at midnight for the next day's events, so that when we got up next morning we would know what the programme was. They were good people to be with, former top-line athletes who knew the pressures and the priorities.

Nick, to use an old fashioned description, is an absolute gent, you never hear him raise his voice, while Lynn's big-time experience and Welsh humour were invaluable. Athletes don't need motivating at an Olympics, they need all irritations in their paths smoothed out for them, an understanding of idosyncrasies, an acceptance that we are all different. Mary, too, was all these things, tremendously caring and emotional. At one stage Russian officials tried to stop Linsey McDonald from going out for the 4 × 400 metres relay medal ceremony because she had the wrong tracksuit bottom, and Mary rushed round to find something – far too large – which little Linsey had to roll up five times, but it got her out there.

I had the usual early-morning run before the final, my stomach had cleared and the problem was now out of my mind. I sensed the Village was beginning to buzz about the race, that not many people thought I could do it but they wanted to be there. I'd heard what the bookies' odds were at home. When I was told they were 11 to 4 on Steve I smiled, it could have been something out of *The Sting,* as if I had deliberately thrown the 800 metres, in order to shift a pile on to the 1,500 metres! How could the odds be that short on a two-horse race? George had sent me a telegram after the 800 metres: 'The bookies have retired, now for your Number One event.' If a knowledgeable critic such as Rodda says I'm not going to win, that's fair enough, but I felt the bookies' odds were ridiculous. It acted as an additional spur.' **)**

I met Seb after an early lunch and wandered down to the almost deserted training track on the fringe of the Village. The only other person there was a large, hirsute Bulgarian girl swimmer in a bikini bottom. Brendan had delivered his last pep-talk to Seb: 'Win this, and you can go on to take the lot in the future, the 5,000 metres and even the 10,000 metres. The other guy can win it, of course, but you can go out there and piss it. There's no way he can do that. But lose it, and you could be finished.' We were sitting on white plastic chairs under a sunshade. Seb was so at ease we could have been back home in the garden. I slipped him a succession of casual, conversational questions about his condition, his conviction, his tactics. I asked him if there was any single aspect of the race that he feared. The answers, though equally casual, were unhesitating. I knew then he was ready for probably the most important race he would ever have to run.

More than at any time in the past week he was at one with himself. For months I had observed the Himalayan effort, dedication and self-denial which had gone into preparing for this moment. I knew the extent of his self-motivation, and now he was convinced that he could do to his great rival what Ovett had so unerringly done to others for the last three years: stay close to the pace-maker, in touch whatever the speed, and strike on the final bend. I said to him that a few minutes of physical or mental pain this afternoon would be worth the enduring glory. He looked up and simply said: 'Why not?' Peter arrived and joined us. He re-emphasized that if Seb stayed with the pace right at the front, the only way he could lose was by being boxed. His last, pragmatic instruction was, 'if necessary – punch!'

❝ I was well aware that there was more pressure on me in this race than in any I had ever run, but I felt good. As we walked through the security exit gate of the Village, the inevitable hand-held camera crews homed in, the luckless interviewers going through the boring routine questions – How do you see it? Interesting. Are you confident? Yes. Can you win it? Yes. Have you seen Steve today? No. The same old stuff. I wondered how they would ever get it back to London before the race was already over. Even our Russian car driver, who took us down to the stadium, was more switched on than usual, enquiring in broken English: 'Ovut good? You vin?' grinning and showing his gold fillings. It wasn't like the 800 metres: I was alive, I just wanted to get down there and get on with it, get finished with Moscow and the Games as soon as I could. ❞

After I left Seb at the training track, I met David Shaw outside the

Village and we jumped into a taxi to head back to the Rossiya where he was also based, for a change of clothes in the sweltering heat before setting off for the stadium and the climax of the Games, including the marathon. As we crossed the Moscva River and headed for the centre of the city, we ran into chaos. The Russians, reacting as in so many instances with over-efficiency, had closed all roads approaching the river-bank marathon course about two hours before it was necessary, with the result that even Moscow's moderately congested traffic was already paralysed and at a horn-blowing, fist-waving, radiator-boiling standstill. Even though our cab driver rose to the occasion with a burst of improvisation which broke every rule in the police manual, he was stumped. We tried every back double, failed abysmally to bribe our way through police road blocks with official British team lapel badges, and even though going the wrong way down several one-way streets were finally forced to abandon the taxi and run the last half mile to the Rossiya. David Shaw immediately telephoned the Village to make sure that British competitors allowed themselves plenty of time to get down to the stadium.

❙ I knew the aggression which had been lacking in the 800 metres was back for the 1,500 metres when I used appalling language to two guards who tried to cut off the approach to the warm-up track because of the marathon, which had just begun. When we got out on to the track in the Lenin Stadium after the warm up, the British supporters had built up a tremendous noise, chanting the names of Steve and me. This race was for them. I don't remember too much of the preliminaries, my mental cutout following the warm up was this time working properly. Steve and I and young Steve Cram all wished each other luck. Ovett said to me, 'give it stick' in a friendly way, and suggested we should have a drink together after the race. He seemed confident. ❩

The sun beat down. The tension was electric. Our first glimpse of the runners was in their tracksuits among the guards at the entrance to the tunnel. Zdravkovic was the first to appear, then the powerfully muscled Straub, then Seb in a grey top, followed by Ovett, frowning as he came out into the sunlight. Suddenly the order was given and like a pack of foxhounds they broke away down the back straight for the final, statutory warm up. Seb did several stooping exercises to stretch his hamstring, then turned in front of the huge contingent of East German supporters at the end of the back straight, and ran back side by side with Ovett towards the tunnel. As they went, they passed the Nero-like figure of Andy Norman, standing alone in shirt sleeves with arms folded, down in one of the photographers' dug-outs. At last the nine finalists, stripped and sleek, were led single file towards the start, now on an invisible leash. They lined up, jostled, regrouped – and the gun went. Straub and Seb went straight to the front, with the blond Plachy at the back of the group.

❛ It was a pedestrian pace but there was very little bargeing for such a slow procession. Jurgen ran just ahead of me, always with his head down as if he were looking for marks on the track, but he was locked into his own private world, he knew what he had come to do. I was very relaxed, completely free of worry, though others may have thought that I was once more playing into Steve's hands. ❜

As they came off the first bend into the home straight they were grouped in twos: Straub and Coe, Marajo and Ovett, Cram and Busse, Fontanella and Zdravkovic. On they went, cautious, contained. Down the second back straight Cram had moved up alongside Ovett, ahead of Marajo. Other than that, there was no change as the pack, still unbroken, moved sedately to the 800 metres mark in 2:04·9. It was now that Straub made the move which would convert the race from a stroll into a remorseless burn all the way to the tape.

❛ Suddenly I realized Straub was going for broke, I knew that no one could take over that kind of pace, not that they would want to. I had to follow Jurgen, and I guessed instinctively that Steve would be tracking me so as to have both of us in his sights. He would know that I was the one to follow, that Jurgen had sacrificed his final kick by making his bid so far from home. When Jurgen went, he opened up daylight and I had to fasten on very quick – and it just kept getting quicker. I felt comfortable.

120

Suddenly it was single file, and I was running free in a lane of my own. I knew that sustained speed of this sort would play into my hands. I'd always been confident, arrogant if you like, that I could maintain that speed longer than anyone. I was out on the Rivelin Valley Road again, but this time it was Jurgen's back ahead of me and not my father's car. *And* I was in a position to break first. **)**

From the dawdle of the first two laps, 61·6 for the first followed by 63·3, Jurgen Straub had lifted the third to a searing 54·6. Up in the stands, Peter was convinced the race was as good as over. 'No one in the world can keep that speed the way Seb can. It didn't look fast, because the front three were all such superb stylists.' At the bell, the order had been, strung out in line: Straub, Coe, Ovett, Busse, Fontanella, Marajo, with Cram trying to hold on in seventh position. Into the back straight for the last time the order remained the same. Ovett, the television commentators were saying as if in unison, was poised for victory.

(At the 1,200 metres mark Straub dug his head down again for a final assault and I had to respond. Going into the final bend I was right on his shoulder. Down the back straight I'd been conscious that we were coming to the physical climax of the race, that I was going to have to give it everything. I knew that the previous 600 metres would have softened everyone behind. We were into an area where we were no longer middle distance runners, where the hours of conditioning in training were needed: 'sprint, drive, work the arms'. I put in a semi-kick at 180 metres, and that carried me past Jurgen, there was daylight and I could hear his feet receding. **)**

What Seb did not know was that his kick had almost exactly coincided with Ovett's bid to overtake *him,* and now Ovett saw the gap between them stretch to another stride and a half. The 'split' times would show that Seb was actually accelerating the whole way from 180 metres to 50 metres out.

❮ I put in another semi-kick coming off the bend and took two glances back down either side. Jurgen was still just in vision inside, with Steve right in line behind him so that I couldn't see him. I was now running for the tape, the mental agony of knowing I had hit my limit, of not knowing what was happening back there behind me. I was not to know they were fading too. I tried to drive again at 40 metres out, and in the next few strides I knew I had nothing left if anyone came back at me. The anxiety over the last 20 metres was unbearable, and it showed in my face as I crossed the line. After a few yards I sank down onto my knees. When I watched that display on the replay it was a bit embarrassing, but it was such a bloody marvellous relief. **❯**

Seb had won the gold medal with a last 800 metres of 1:48·5, the fastest last two laps ever run in a three-and-a-half or four-lap race. The last 300 metres had been covered in 39, the last 200 metres in 24·7, the last 200 metres in 12·1! His winning time of 3:38·4 might be over six seconds outside his world record, but who cared?

On a street in the middle of Liverpool Seb's closest friend at Loughborough, Sean Butler, a middle distance man who had shared countless long hours grinding out the miles on the road in winter, and whose gentle wit and relaxed nature had contributed much towards maintaining a normal balance in his companion's pressurized life, was watching the race in the window of a TV retailer. He was one of a large crowd which had gathered, and at the end of the first lap he had exclaimed, 'Christ, Ovett looks good'. Thereafter he had managed to keep his thoughts to himself, even when that final glorious run for home began. In the hubbub on the pavement after the finish, another Liverpudlian turned to Sean and said: 'I don't know what you're smiling about. You wanted Ovett to win!'

❮ I remember going off on my lap of honour and having to side step the blazer brigade. I'd won – and I flipped. I didn't know what I was doing. I couldn't believe it would feel the way it did. It wouldn't have been half as good, as acute, if I hadn't gone through the previous few days. They were dreadful days. I'd bottled it all up, and now the emotion was coming out like champagne that had been shaken. I put my arm round Steve, but it was all reflex. As I ran down the back straight, the one great overriding feeling was that I was free, 'I don't need this hassle any more, I don't have to put up with the aggro if I don't want to'. To have that kind of feeling so soon, a psychologist might say that I had actually lost some of the joy of running, and for a short while I would probably have agreed. I just hadn't realized the extent of the pressure. Yet thirty minutes later I was in the press conference and talking about moving up to the 5,000 metres in 1984. I knew I could now retire at any point and feel a satisfied man. Not that I'd achieved everything which was possible, far from it, there were more world records to break, more gold medals to win, but could they ever mean as much? It had never been my intention to go on racing indefinitely. **)**

The praise now heaped upon Seb exceeded even the criticism of the previous week. Ian Wooldridge wrote on the front page of the *Daily Mail*:

> 'Coe did more than win the gold medal. He lifted the soul, he ennobled his art, he dignified his country . . . Watching him run, invincible, over the last 300 metres was unforgettable. Watching him afterwards made you even prouder, for his conduct in triumph matched his humility in disaster . . . He wasn't here to settle some parochial feud by incinerating Steve Ovett. For six days he had had to live with himself for running so far below his intellect in the 800 metres and losing to Ovett that his only challenger yesterday was himself.'

In *The Times* Norman Fox reported:

> 'Once bitten, but not twice shy . . . it was pride as much as medals and records that were at issue and this time Coe refused to be driven into awkward situations in the longer, more studied race. This was Ovett's first defeat in forty-six races. There was no question that it was done without room for further debate, and at the end he accepted it with the grace that some people doubted was in his soul.'

Peter Hildreth who, in the previous week's *Sunday Telegraph* had stated that Coe had no chance on earth, now called it 'a sublime finale' and added:

123

'Coe was timed over the last 800 metres in 1:48·8 – fast enough to earn a passage for several runners through the heats of the 800 metres. It was treatment like this meted out by Pekka Vasala of Finland which proved the undoing of the great Kip Keino in the Munich 1,500 metres final in 1972. It was also too much for Ovett. Though the flowing rhythm was held, Ovett had no upper register when Coe made his move off the final turn. And Coe's winning two-stage kick was no ad lib invention.'

❝ When I finally ran off the track after the lap of honour, I accidently ran hard into Ron Pickering, there with a microphone, and almost knocked him over. 'How does it feel?' he asked. All I could reply was, 'Oh, Christ', which subsequently earned me a sharp reprimand from the Bishop of Durham. In the background Mike Murphy was saying 'bloody magic, bloody magic'. As we waited in the dope-testing room, we were asked by a Russian official if we would attend the press conference. Straub and I said yes, Steve said no, and added, 'I'm surprised you're going, after the stick you've been given these last five days'. I laughed and truthfully said I hadn't seen it, though I knew about it; I was surprised that the guy who was supposed to be indifferent to the press was in fact so sensitive. As we stood around waiting for the doping formalities – 'are these your two samples, sign the labels please, initial the corks please' – Steve said to me, 'it takes a bit of time to sink in doesn't it?' I replied, 'well, we've both been losers out here, and we've both sacrificed a lot in our lives to be winners'. After a while Steve said, 'I don't know, do you think the sacrifice is worth all this. I begin to wonder.' I just wondered if he would have said that if he'd won. Yet there's a streak in me which was glad he didn't go back home with nothing, because I knew exactly how I would have felt.

The rest of the evening was chaos, one endless succession of television studios. Brasher leaped into a car with us to go to the television studios the other side of Moscow, to complete his story for Sunday. ITV arranged a link-up with my mother in the YTV studios in Leeds, but it got delayed while Peter and John Walker, who was in the London studio with Dickie Davies, became involved in a four-minute discussion on tactics, until Davies finally said, 'you must be waiting to speak to your wife'. My mother looked a trifle smashed, and was certainly very happy!

When Peter said goodbye he added, 'and go carefully on my Scotch', absolutely dead-pan. Probably half the population back home thought he was serious: he'd had a go at his son, now it was his wife! As we left the studios, approaching midnight, Brasher said that he was going to be running in the New York marathon. I told him my letter would be in the post. **'**

More than twenty million people in Britain had watched that hypnotic three-and-a-half minute race on TV – stopping work in the office or factory, standing in the street to watch in retailers' windows, even taking the afternoon off. They were drawn by the magnetism of one slim young runner and his race with himself, as much as with his brilliant arch-rival. Derek Johnson, 1956 silver medallist at 800 metres and Chairman of the International Athletes Club, summed up succinctly: 'It was the greatest finish to a 1,500 metres since Jack Lovelock's in 1936. To kick twice at that pace was something I had not believed possible.' When Seb arrived home, such was the crush of well-wishers and press and photographers at London Airport that police sealed off the M4 system for several minutes to permit him to show a clean pair of heels for the second time in three days.

9: Freedom

Leni Riefenstahl's film of the Nazi Olympics in Berlin in 1936 exposed all their prophetic military overtones. What we saw in the closing ceremony of the 1980 Olympic Games in Moscow was equally ominous. It may be that the western world, for all its current misgivings, is not as vulnerable to a power bid from a nation with acute international, political and economic problems as Europe was in 1935-9, but there was no mistaking the message of Soviet might which was relayed to the world at that ceremony. The mood may have been lightened with decorative folk dancing, but the massive exhibition of synchronized gymnastic efficiency was symbolic of the domination of the individual by the state. And the three supreme leaders of the armed forces, whose images were interwoven into the display, possessed three of the hardest faces I think I have ever seen. It was with a shudder, not a song, that I left the stadium with Peter at the conclusion.

Seb has stated with clarity his reasons for believing that the British did right to oppose the boycott advocated by their government. I find myself in an ambivalent position, believing on the one hand that the boycott was morally right, but that the government forfeited their case, and swung the majority of the population against them, by presenting it so clumsily and insincerely. There is probably little disparity between my standpoint and Seb's, and I think my post-Olympic attitude was perfectly set out in the following leader in *The Times*:

'There were several ideas behind the attempt to boycott the Moscow Olympics. The main one was that the Soviet Union should be denied the propaganda advantage which it hoped to reap from the Games. In many statements the Soviet Union had made it clear that the Games were to be presented not only as a sort of coming-out party at which the world, by attending, would be recognizing the success and respectability of the Soviet Union, but also as a specific endorsement of Soviet "peace

126

policy" abroad. In other words the Games were to be a highly political event designed to further Soviet policies and win support for them.

'This was, of course, true from the moment the Games were awarded to Moscow, but at that time many felt that the propaganda advantage to the Soviet Union would be outweighed by the benefits of diminishing the isolation which contributes to some of the less desirable aspects of Soviet policy. After Afghanistan, the balance swung the other way. It was rightly felt that to grant the Soviet Union a specific endorsement of its foreign policy while it was killing people in occupied Afghanistan would be morally abhorrent and politically unwise. The fact that the boycott was, in the end, patchy in its execution and limited in its effects does not mean that the attempt was wrong or not worthwhile. To have tried and partly failed is much better than not to have tried at all. In only one respect does the partial boycott seem to have been a total failure. As far as can be ascertained, the broad masses of the Soviet people got the wrong message or none at all. Most seem to believe that Soviet forces are in Afghanistan to help. They attribute the boycott to American ill-will, and if they are angry it is not at Mr Brezhnev but at Mr Carter. This is a pity but it does not invalidate the attempt.'

⟨ As I have said earlier, I think it was necessary for the British to insist on their participation in the Games in order to ensure that international sport should not be wrecked for all time, and should not become fair game for any politicians looking for a platform. Having made my own decision to go, it is impossible for me to say with hindsight how I might have felt if I'd lost both races. Maybe my mother was near the mark when she asked after the 800 metres if I was thinking of retiring. Certainly my career would have been at the cross-roads, yet I like to think that the same thing which churned me up, made me get off my backside and win the 1,500 metres, would have reacted again if I'd lost that. But at what level? Besides, I still consider even now that the Olympics are *not* necessarily a true test of ability. If I'd gone there only for the 800 metres, would the result have meant that I was second best in the world and in Britain? I don't honestly think so. I was often asked before the Games whether I would swop my world record for an Olympic gold medal. I found it difficult to answer. I think the records of 1979 were in fact the truer indication of athletic ability. **)**

During the winter of 1980-1 Seb re-aligned his training towards quality rather than the stamina-producing work of the winter of 1979-80, which was geared to the endurance of six races in twelve days in Moscow. During that winter he once again became a part-time athlete, concentrating at the same time on his post-graduate course at Loughborough. Yet he found that under this arrangement his academic life was still compromised.

(University lecturers and tutors in my first three years considered it insulting if you were not prepared to devote your whole being to their pursuit. I'm not asking for degrees to become mickey-mouse, half-hour oral tests, but universities should provide a student with more than a degree. Under the syllabus at Loughborough I've never fully expanded my mental curiosity. I've cut corners horribly because of athletics. I would have been far happier had I stayed with economic history rather than economics. I was not at ease with the staff, who could only see my outside commitments as devaluing their own purpose. I have found some academics extremely narrow. The day of the rounded man has gone; the British university system is not producing the properly developed, thinking person.

I'm grateful for the added experience athletics has given me even if in some ways it has limited my activities. To an extent it is unnerving to have become public property, it has cut down the number of places I can go to have a normal day out. Unless I go through the turnstiles and stand on the terraces at football matches, there is always the likelihood that I may be asked to make a presentation or something at half-time or after the game, which is perfectly pleasant but you are no longer a private person. I have girlfriends, but mostly no one special – partly because I haven't the time for a close relationship outside the family, but also, with a girl, I have to be so careful that casual remarks are not taken out of context by others. In Sheffield it's almost impossible for me to be seen with a girl, even though she may not even be a personal friend of mine. The press take so many liberties. I've been called a 'cad' in front-page headlines in a Sunday

During weight training such as this, Seb will lift up to twenty times his own body weight of 9 stone 7 pounds in order to build endurance (above) *Daily Mail*

High in the Peak District above Sheffield, the lonely record-breaker pounds the deserted road during one of his regular ten-mile runs (below)

Vainly Seb tries to make up the lost ground on his arch rival, Steve Ovett, as they battle towards the tape with East German Detlef Wagenknecht (fifth) at the end of the 800m *The Associated Press Ltd*

(Opposite) Four phases on the way to the 1,500m gold medal. Top: at **200m** Straub (338) has the lead, which he held for three-quarters of the race. Behind, on the inside, is Cram (257); Coe is running wide and obscures Marajo (243), with Ovett (279) obscuring Plachy (783) and Fontanella (426), and Busse (296) running wide beside Ovett. Top centre: at **600m** the three Britons are relaxed, behind Straub, with Zdravkovic (767) bringing up the rear of the nine-man field. Bottom centre: at **1,000m** Straub suddenly begins his long burst for home and Coe and Ovett respond instantly. Bottom: into the final straight, at **1,400m**, Coe makes his second 'kick' to take Straub, leaving Ovett and Busse (obscured) two and three strides adrift *Chris Smith/Sunday Times*

200m

600m

1,000m

1,400m

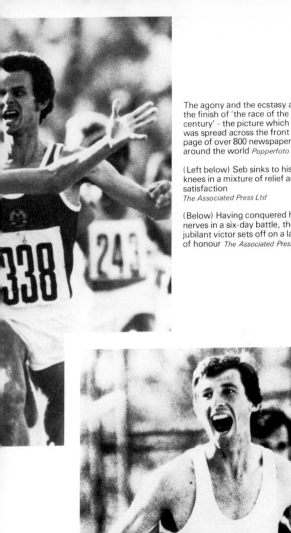

The agony and the ecstasy at the finish of 'the race of the century' - the picture which was spread across the front page of over 800 newspapers around the world *Popperfoto*

(Left below) Seb sinks to his knees in a mixture of relief and satisfaction
The Associated Press Ltd

(Below) Having conquered his nerves in a six-day battle, the jubilant victor sets off on a lap of honour *The Associated Press Ltd*

'We've done it!' The 1,000m record falls again *Daily Express*

'If only I'd known the lap times!' Dismay at missing Ovett's 1,500m record by a fraction after running 'blind' in Stockholm *Daily Express*

'Come on, my son!' Peter implores Seb to raise a last-ditch gallop in order to rescue a fading attempt on the mile record in Zurich *Daily Express*

Who's going to take second? Effort and concentration among the rest as Seb coasts towards an 800m Europa Cup victory in Helsinki
The Associated Press Ltd

The Pied Piper of Oslo. An eager young audience salute Seb's fourth Bislett world record (in the 1,000m)
Daily Express

Tom Byers leads Seb and Mike Boit through the fastest ever first half-mile on route to a sensational new time in the Golden Mile in Brussels *Daily Express*

Seb recommends a life-ban for drug offenders during the first address ever by an athlete to the ICC at the Baden-Baden Congress *Popperfoto*

A Roman holiday. At the conclusion of a momentous season, Seb romps home ahead of James Robinson in the World Cup 800m *The Associated Press Ltd*

newspaper, because I became friends with one girl without, allegedly, telling another girl whom I had known for some while. She, unjustifiably, claimed I should have let her know. Much of what was said in the paper was a gross distortion of the truth, but in that kind of situation I am obliged to stay silent. There is an intolerable intrusion by press and photographers into my private life, waiting outside my house or digs all night and inventing 'quotes'. I sometimes resort to the disguise of dark glasses and hat at football matches and airports. **❭**

Even his own fans, however well meaning, try to take him over at times. Particularly in the north, there is a feeling that if you become famous then it must be partly due to the fact that you are from the north; that you are part of some gigantic northern free-masonry and that therefore your success belongs not just to you, but to the region. At a Bradford boxing evening where Seb was a guest, he was sitting signing autographs almost continuously from seven till midnight. At one point an elderly man came up to him and, not unfriendly, said, ' 'ere lad, tha's 'ad thi free meal, nah git thi naame dahn on theer', shoving forward a menu. He is 'our' Seb. Passing in the street, a lady remarked to him, 'it's nice to have something in Sheffield that no one else has'. Some*thing*. At his second civic reception by the mayor and corporation after the Olympics – the first followed the records, the most lavish and glittering sporting social occasion in Sheffield's history – he spent the better part of two hours graciously saying hello to everyone who mattered, civic, industrial, and union dignitaries, signing autographs and making an impromptu speech, and at the finish he was the *only* person present in the city hall who had not had anything to eat!

When he returned after the Golden Mile in 1979, there was a note waiting from a local athletic organization advising him, in all seriousness, 'if you don't get your entry form in you won't be able to run, we've warned you about this before'. He can be excused for feeling at times that Sheffield is not so much a mother to him as a mother-in-law. Yet his loyalty is strongly to the north: Yorkshire, not Crystal Palace, is his 'home', a fact which people who write even to me complaining if he is absent from a fixture in London do not understand. In 1980 he ran in more domestic events prior to the Games than almost any other Moscow

129

competitor: the Yorkshire championships, the Northern Counties, the Inter-Counties, an international, and the U.K. Closed. And after the Games he cancelled a pre-arranged run in Berlin in order to appear in the Coca-Cola at Crystal Palace. He is patriotic as far as he is able to be where internationals and the Europa Cup are concerned, but critical of discipline among the team when abroad.

❬ The situation has improved considerably with the introduction of team managers who know what they are doing, there is no comparison, for instance, between Prague in 1978 and Turin and Zagreb in 1979 and 1981. But the fact is that there is still a bit of a folklore hangover about high jinks on these trips from days gone by. Some members of the team take the attitude that it is one big carousel. You find athletes playing dominoes till four in the morning, coming in late from discos, playing stereo tapes and radios until all hours, and keeping others awake.

When somebody like Wells or Capes or Foster or me complains that we're trying to sleep in the afternoon, that's not being awkward, it's because that's our routine: not playing frisbee in the corridor. On every trip we go on there are those who joke about the East Germans or Russians never being seen at the discos, but that's the name of the game. The ones who denigrate the East German system are the same ones who cannot wait for the next trip abroad to have a good time, who live their lives vicariously through athletics, and are not prepared to give the sport what it really needs to succeed. You have to have discipline, and the sort of enthusiasm which Geoff Capes has always given. No one has competed in more internationals than Geoff, no one is more patriotic, he's a tremendous team man. He's very out-spoken and that's why he was often in trouble with the Board, but of all the recent British athletes, he's the one I would be happy to see as team manager. With him there would be discipline. ❭

Towards the end of the season a couple of years ago Seb gave Peter an experimental scare. He had been feeling lethargic, and as they went off for an evening training stint he said casually that he had been to the doctor to get a pick-me-up and that he was 'souped up' for the evening. Peter went pale, and there was a pause while he considered if Seb was being serious – until his son grinned.

‘ Until I was nineteen or twenty I was rather naïve. I didn't really know what was financially possible in athletics. Yet now, Daley can say that ultimately he wants to be a millionaire, and a child can pick up a paper and read that Ed Moses has received £1,500 for a race in Italy. So the danger is that if a young athlete discovers that drugs can be a short-cut to success and material reward, why should be turn them down? That does not apply just to world champions, but to club runners wanting to move up from the second team to the first, for county runners wanting to become internationals. I know of British athletes who have experimented with drugs, though I have never been tempted and never would be. Yet I am low enough down the distance range – towards the sprint end – for them to be potentially useful. Fortunately I've been able to win without them. But if a coach said to you that in judicious doses it could do something startling for you, would you submit? The stupidity is, of course, that, in the end, you get a situation in which *everyone* is on a medical back-up, the difference between first and third is still going to come down to training and character, the human factor. I admire Christine Benning, a leading women's middle distance runner, but I think she was misguided to take a stand on drugs as a reason for not going to the Olympics, where she knew the Eastern Europeans would all be on additives. It would have been better if she had gone, and had been able to say *she* got into the last eight *without* taking drugs. That would have been something to build on. The difference between a women's 800 metres in 1:53 and 1:55 is probably medical, but drugs can become a cop-out for British women. I believe with proper coaching and application there are British women who could get down to 1:55/1:56. I suspect that the right distance for Linsey MacDonald is 800 metres, and that if she does not get a medal in 1984 or 1988 it is more likely to be because of factors other than drugs, factors we all face. Her small size need not necessarily be a limitation at the highest level. At five feet nine inches and just over nine stone, I was able to break the world record for 800 metres, yet there is no text book which says that I ought to be able to do this, and I'm sure that's why I have been drug tested so often. Linsey reached

131

an Olympic final at sixteen and there is no reason why, with careful development, she shouldn't make a very talented 800 metres runner. I will be disappointed if she doesn't eventually do something big. **)**

Twelve days after his gold medal, Seb was back in the mountains at Macolin in Switzerland, preparing for an attack on his 1,500 metres world record. The weather was glorious, and he spent several relaxing days running in the woods, and we had a superb fish meal down beside Lake Neuchâtel, watching the surf sailors skimming the water until the only light was from the hotels and houses winking along the lakeside. But his hamstring was increasingly troublesome and needed constant attention. We drove down to Zürich for the race; Peter and Angela had flown in that afternoon. Peter passed him the lap times he thought would do it – 55·5, 1:51·5 (56), 2:48·0 (56·5), 3:30 (42). The field would include Walker, Bayi, Scott, and Coghlan, with Flynn making the early pace. Would anyone be able to push him over the third lap as Straub had done in Moscow?

On a cool evening Flynn took the field through the first lap ahead of schedule in 54·3, with Seb close on his heels, followed by the big four. At 800 metres they had slowed to 1:52·5, a second outside Peter's planned time. Too late Seb tried to pick up the third lap, and the 1,200 metres was passed in 2:51·5, three and a half seconds slow. Although Seb put in a 40·6 last 300 metres, ripping clear of Walker and Scott around the final turn, he failed by a fraction, with a time of 3:32·19, to equal the record he shared with Ovett. It was over six seconds faster than his winning time in Moscow, the then third fastest 1,500 metres ever run. He was nonetheless disappointed. Even more so when he arrived home, after losing by inches to Don Paige in Viareggio, and it was diagnosed that the sciatic trouble was due to the tilt in his pelvis. He had won the gold medal running with one leg a quarter of an inch shorter than the other and now he would have to have a complete layoff, cancelling further planned races in Brussels and Leicester, the latter a mile where he had intended to try to get back that record. He was also a non-starter in the 1980 Golden Mile, this time run at Crystal Palace and won by Ovett with a late burst clear of Scott in 3:52·84. Ovett had failed with a double bid at both 1,500 metres and the mile in Brussels, but running once more at the end of a crowded, eventful season, at Koblenz on 27 August, he improved his and Seb's 1,500 metres record by 0·7 to 3:31·36. The vital factor was that Ovett was taken through the critical third lap in 57·7, for a 1,200 metres time of 2:50·7, by Tom Wessinghage, the West German doctor who had missed the Olympic 5,000 metres because of the boycott, and now ran 3:31·6 himself, also to beat the record.

❛ The greatest reward of the gold medal was that it freed me to do what I enjoy, to lay about the record books in 1981 without the accusation that I was trying to justify myself in the only way I could. I wanted to go out last summer, not bothering about splits and pace-makers, and just do it myself as I did in 1979. The Olympics got in the way of that. They impose false restrictions. Throughout the winter of 1979-80 I was thinking of a span of six races in nine days, rather than a one-off blinder. Of course, I finished up with a gold and a silver, and another world record, but it interrupted what I really enjoy doing. In 1981 I hoped not just to nibble the records but to improve them substantially. What I really want from athletics is an 800 metres in under 1:41, a 1,500 metres in under 3:30 and a mile in under 3:46. I did my bit in 1980 in satisfying those who react primarily to the Olympics every four years, and unfairly rate an athlete's status exclusively by that performance. There have been some great athletes who never achieved anything in the Olympics. I enjoy running for myself, for the pure fun and exhilaration of running at speeds that have not been run before. The Coe who crossed the line in Zürich in 1979 or Brussels in 1981 would have been fifty yards past the tape in Moscow. ❜

Late in 1979, Seb, as one of the dozen chief guests, attended the Man of the Year luncheon at the Savoy in London, a dignified charity function chaired by the Duke of Devonshire. Those being honoured beside the young runner who had broken three world records were men of letters, of valour, of research, of medicine. There was also disc jockey and radio presenter Jimmy Young. Seb sat back and listened to Frank Bough, the master of ceremonies, cite the accomplishments which had brought these men together: a famous physicist; a man who had reached the height of esteem in medicine in spite of being unable to read and write as a teenager because of dyslexia; a lifeboatman of unimaginable courage who was the first in history to win bronze, silver, and gold medals for gallantry; a policeman who had arrested armed raiders, been shot in the stomach and crawled to ring for help; a fireman who had held burning timbers while a colleague was rescued; an army captain who had lost both legs in Northern Ireland and was back on active service. Towards the end of the citation Seb and Jimmy Young caught each other's eyes, and Jimmy leaned over to say exactly what was also in Seb's mind: 'What on earth am I doing here?'

❝ I've never been so impressed with a group of people in my life. It was a lesson, it really did bring me back down to earth. It made me think how easy it is to become a household name, a well-known face, for doing very little in terms of general ability. We put a strange premium on fame in this country these days, it seems to me. People are famous merely for being well known, rather than for the true merit of what they have achieved. What I've done is not outstanding in anything other than the field in which I'm operating; and therefore I feel embarrassed about standing up in chat shows and such like and giving opinions on art, politics, or economics – subjects which I might feel I know a little bit about but not to the extent that I should impose my views on a vast audience. It's not false modesty, I just don't see the point unless somebody wants me specifically to discuss sport. I do what I do in athletics not just for the satisfaction of the world record or the gold medal, but to plumb the depths of myself and discover what my potential is as a person. But it surprises me that people are interested in a sportsman's views on unrelated subjects. I suppose that's the price of success!

Anybody should attempt to excel at whatever they do, but the measure of their success should not only be the public estimation of what they achieve, which has fixed stereotypes, but how close they come to their own potential. That is why, depending on your potential, it is possible to retire from athletics, say, with much less than an Olympic gold medal and be really satisfied. What was so crushing for me in Moscow when I lost the 800 metres was that I knew I had fallen so wretchedly short of my true ability. ❞

10: Faster Still

The general public, although it has a certain vague awareness of the relevance of training for the world's leading athletes, has no concept of what it actually means to fulfil training schedules for at least 325 days of the year. Most people have an idea of something they would term 'going for a run', rather as a senior executive of the Chase Manhattan Bank might get up early twice a week in his Mayfair apartment and go for a jog in Hyde Park, before strolling down to his office in Berkeley Square after an orange-juice-and-toast breakfast. I have a close friend, interested in sport as a keen spectator who, until recently, supposed that men such as Coe would be able to ease up in the winter and only begin again in earnest in the spring like, say, a county cricketer. Yet for the foremost runners, racing comes almost as relief from training, that grinding process of conditioning which continues inexorably and unbroken from one season into the next, with perhaps a three- or four-week break at most. I have been to a social event with Seb in winter, long after the cheering has become the faintest echo and months since the television video clips have been put away, when he has been unable to sit comfortably at the dinner table because of soreness in the ham-strings following a severe session in the gymnasium with the weights.

❢ The biggest incentive to get back into training in the late autumn of 1980 was that I seriously considered it had been a poor season. It's difficult even now to be articulate about it, but neither Peter nor I could be satisfied. Other than the 1,000 metres record, I had not run *faster*, which has to be the aim. It doesn't matter what the year brings you in the way of titles, the objective is to improve. Yet, having said that, I think I grew up mentally that year. Being sidelined for five or six weeks with the pelvic injury was probably a blessing in disguise. When you are used to daily training, five weeks is a long time, and when I began again it was a relief not to have pain, which had been there almost the whole year. I cannot say enough for the treatment of Terry Moule, who successfully manipulated my lower back and pelvis to correct the displacement.

I was grateful – and lucky. You have only to think of injuries to other world record holders such as Walker and Bedford, which have wrecked whole seasons. I remember saying to Peter at the height of the injury that it was easy to get carried away by a gold medal, and that I'd happily exchange it in order to be able to go out running again free of injury. Mentally it can be very depressing. Suddenly you are brought down to earth when you realize other people have been finished by a lot less. It was a really dreadful period, wondering how I would come out of it, and the pain killers depressed me even more. Yet the fact that my last race of the season had ended in defeat acted as a spur, and it was ironic that the guy who beat me, Don Paige, himself spent most of 1981 out of action with a knee injury. I had to remind myself continually that there was a great deal more to be done, even though I had a gold and silver medal and, as in previous years, had learned more about myself. **9**

It would have been possible for Seb, being the main attraction, to have asked the Italian organizers to shift Paige to a different event in Viareggio. But that is not his style. In spite of his injury and the knowledge that Paige, absent from Moscow because of the American boycott, was a serious rival, Seb fulfilled his obligation: and was beaten by inches. What did slightly rile him was that the American *Track and Field News* proceeded to rank Paige number one for the year on account of this single race when, in fact, Seb had twice run faster that season, for Loughborough and in the Northern Counties Championships back in June.

6I don't want to sound complaining but another problem that autumn was the social side of life. If I thought the demands on my time were pretty substantial in 1979, they were nothing compared with what happened in 1980. It's all down to the business of what the public feel about Olympic gold medals. The requests for appearances were two- or three-fold, and I had no idea of the extent to which the public's interest would be raised even further. That success removes you from being well known merely for your sport, it becomes a passport for an invitation to functions in no way connected with sport. Sure, one travels the world free in the summer, and I love going to Scandinavia and Italy, but now I found myself in a situation where I was actually made to feel I was inconveniencing people by not making myself available! To cap it all, my year ended with the newspapers being full of a speeding offence, with my friends and family finding out even before I knew myself. There were moments such as this when I longed to disappear from the public eye. 〉

His first race after the injury was in December, cross-country at Osterley Park running a three-mile relay leg for Loughborough, followed by the Hyde Park road relays after Christmas. Towards the end of January he won the AAA indoor 3,000 metres at Cosford, and was asked to run for the UK against East Germany a couple of weeks later. Racing indoors over 800 metres for the first time since winning the European title in San Sebastian four years before in 1:46·5 – his first international success – Seb now erased Carlo Grippo's world indoor record by 0.4 seconds with 1:46·0. He was up against Busse and Wagenknecht, fifth and sixth in the Olympic 800 metres and known to be in sharp racing form. Mike Whittingham led the first lap as planned in 25·4, and Seb went to the front at the half-way (52·3) followed by Busse. With a characteristic burst in the finishing straight he ripped clear of the German for a result which was the perfect augury to the summer which lay ahead – the first world record by a Briton at home since Dave Bedford's 10,000 metres in 1973.

〈 I had no thought of going for a record until just before the race. I knew I was fit, but I didn't think I was in that kind of shape. I'd done a little bit of speed work along lamp-lit pavements in between the basic routine of gym work and distance running. More important than the record by far, however, was getting back on the track and having no reaction from the back. That was the crunch. What was also pleasing was that, for the first time, my elder sister Miranda was able to be there for a big race. She was back home from America and with us for Christmas.

Sean was there too to see a world record for the first time. The help I had from him at the beginning of the season was unbelievable, and invaluable. Much of the preparation was done at Nottingham at the Harvey Haddon Stadium, in peace and quiet on winter mornings, when the Liverpudlian groundsman's voice would suddenly come singing eerily across the empty stadium in the middle of a 300 metres because he didn't realize the public address was switched on. Some of the work was on my own, some with Sean. I'd do a 600, he'd join in at 300. He was running just to help me, because he had no special objective, and that was real friendship.

On Peter's own admission, I was thinking more on my own this year, planning my own schedules in the build-up to the outdoor racing season. They weren't *original*, they were the restult of years of working with him. I'd ring him at regular intervals to say what I was doing, but it was a qualified, deliberate attempt by me to do it on my own and get it right, and he probably knew that. 〕

The schedules were on target. In May there was a 400 metres for Loughborough at Crystal Palace in 46·9, a useful 800 metres in the Yorkshire Championships and then, in June, running for England against the United States, Ethiopia and Belgium, an 800 metres in a fast 1:44·06. Peter, keeping a careful but distant eye on things at a time when the recession was demanding his fullest business attentions, was well satisfied. 'We knew that none of the records outdoors, Seb's or Steve's, were so tight that they couldn't be improved. We particularly wanted a good mile out of the summer, and the World Cup 800 metres. It probably hurt him more than it hurt me, the Moscow business, and will always rankle.' Seb anchored the relay in the international with an impressive 45·7, and four days later travelled to Gateshead to run in the relay against Italy. He drove up the A1 with Bela Domokos, the Hungarian photographer who worked in the laboratories at Loughborough, and had followed Seb around Europe for three seasons. A week later he mysteriously disappeared and has not been seen since, to the consternation of his family and the police.

〈 I spent the Saturday night in Loughborough watching England's soccer victory in Budapest on television, and then drove up with Bela. I walked off the track after the relay to change and fly to London and on to Florence, and it was the last I saw of him. He was a very good photographer, who had just been given the contract for all the International Amateur Athletic Federation Golden Events of that summer, and he was a friend. He'd been at all my world records. I'd helped him a fair bit, I think, in previous years, when he was often a travelling companion and would share my hotel room when he could not get one. It was inexplicable and upsetting that he should just vanish a few days later after giving his daughter a lift into town. **)**

Before Seb flew to Italy, he called me and discussed his prospects, having already spoken to Peter. I wanted to know if there was the slightest chance of a record attempt being 'on'. If so, I would be on the next plane. Just as he had told Peter, he now said to me that he thought the probability slight enough for me not to bother – and like the rest of Fleet Street I missed what was to be something unique among even his exploits!

(I'd wound down my training a bit, I was doing the basic hard-core endurance stuff, although I'd had a personal best 200 metres in well under 22·0. I knew I was in good shape from the 1:44·06 the previous week, but that was all. I arrived at Pisa and made the sticky bus ride to Florence, with the temperature up in the 90s. I don't know if it was a prelude to being ill the following week, but I had a very severe headache before the race. It was so hot that all I could do the day of the race was drink bottled water and try to sleep. Peter and I reckoned that it would be a good warm-up of around 1:43/1:44 and we were looking for a 'safe' run in a warm climate. One of the reasons I didn't expect anything special was that you have to be so on song mentally to run an 800 at world record speed, much more than for four laps. Also, it's not being big-headed, but there is nobody I can discuss the 800 with and say 'what was your build-up?' the way I can with Walker or Coghlan when discussing a 3:49 mile. It's a bit disappointing, in one sense, that there is no one at the moment with whom I can compare notes. **)**

The race was not scheduled until after eleven that night. The American Carl Lewis had had the crowd buzzing with a 100 metres which was flashed up on the screen as 9·91, a new world record, and he proceeded to do five laps of honour, which delayed the start of the 800 metres by over twenty minutes. Seb was in lane 3, with the Yugoslav Zivotic and Grippo, from Italy, immediately outside and the promising young Kenyan, Billy Konchellah, inside. At the lane break Konchellah led, with Seb moving in behind a stride down. Konchellah reached the bell in 49·7, Seb two-tenths behind. Into the bend he was at the Kenyan's shoulder, and surged past him into the back straight.

❛ I could feel the night air was becoming chilled. As I went through the bell I heard Maeve Kyle, the British team manager, shouting '49, 50' so I knew it was fast. I didn't feel as good as in the first record in Oslo in 1979, but that was because I was running half a second faster. The whole of that day I had begun to wonder if the record might be on, but there was no commitment, the weather can change so suddenly in Italy. A week later, for instance, Steve went to Venice and ran his 1,000 metres in an electric storm. When you get to the bell in a record run, which I now knew it could be, the thing that is screaming inside your head is 'keep working'. You know that if you get there in 49-something, the rate of fade is going to be greater than usual. It's going to be hard enough to maintain, but if you lose concentration you know it will be worse. It gets to the point where you are even listening to your own footfalls, dimly trying to discern whether the interval is lengthening. ❜

Down the back straight Seb left Konchellah standing, opening an astonishing 30-metre gap, his arms working with the high piston-like movement of a 200 metre runner, while far back Zivotic moved into second place.

❛ From 420 to 500 metres I was able to lift the pace marginally, but into the final bend I was having to shout at myself mentally to maintain rhythm. One of the most exciting feelings when you are going for a record is when you hit the front, the exhilaration of knowing things are on schedule, the sudden knowledge – like an actor or comedian – that you have your audience on your own, exclusively, all the way to the tape. The response at that moment from the crowd is like nothing else. In a stadium such as Oslo, Brussels, Zürich or Crystal Palace, they know the situation, they know what you are going for, and the reaction coming out of the darkness is a magical moment, a surging push in the back. It rewards the entertainer which I think is there in every top athlete. But as you cross the line there are those split seconds while you wait for the crowd reaction, not looking at the clock, just listening for the noise, the crescendo which tells you have done it, the awful silence, the tailing away which says you've failed. **9**

The first 200 had taken 24·6, the second 25·3. Out on his own, Seb had lifted the third 200 to 25·1, leaving him 27·2 to beat his record of 1:42·33. In fact he covered the final half-lap in 26·7 for an unbelievable 1:41·72. Not since Rudolph Harbig in 1939 had any man been so far ahead of his contemporaries. Seb had lowered the time of Alberto Juantorena by 1·72 seconds, and the average of his five best times was now 1:43·27, faster than any other man had ever run that distance. Juantorena, at his best, would have been 15 yards behind.

6 What was weird was that, as soon as I had finished, they announced a corrected time for Lewis of 10·13. As I lapped the track there was silence, followed by booing. I didn't understand what was happening and thought 'surely it wasn't that bad!' I ran off the track and onto the grass, where Maeve Kyle had 1:41·69 on her watch. She was reluctant to come across and tell me in case she had got it wrong. It appeared that there was a fault with the electronic timing and there was a dreadful ten-minute wait before the official time was confirmed off the photo-finish equipment.

That result gave me more satisfaction than any of the miles and 1,500s. The two 800s, in Oslo and Florence, have been quite different from anything else I've run. Other sportsmen say there are moments when they are outside themselves, watching from the stand, as it were, and I've only experienced that in the 800 metres. The physical and mental effort are so much greater. You accelerate up to a maximum sustainable speed, and just try to hold on to it. There's no luxury of saving anything for a kick, 'I'll ease here and wind up there', so the feeling of release at the finish is always that much greater. Mike Boit always says that 800s are the hardest races on the track. I'd love to have met him at his best. That would have been something. I've always admired and liked him because he is a totally committed runner, neither of us is any good at running defensively. We both agree that it is easier in some ways to run the 800 at top speed rather than under-throttled, even with the mental strain.

It was sad that Peter didn't see it; not only having told him not to bother for Oslo in 1979 but then doing it again in Florence seemed a bit rough. He feels, too, that the 800 and perhaps the 1,000 demand the most of an athlete, a combination of sheer speed and endurance, and it's disappointing for both of us that it doesn't have the cachet of the mile in Britain and America, or the 1,500 in Europe. Usually, you are physiologically born with either the ability to run distance efficiently, or with fast reflex muscles. The 800 demands both, so that it is the hardest to get right in training – the endurance of the 5,000 and the leg speed of a 200 metres runner. The 1,500 is easier, it doesn't call for the same range of ability. **9**

Shortly after the news had been flashed on television back home my phone rang. It was Seb. 'I don't quite know how to tell you this . . . ' And we laughed, because the only thing that mattered at that moment was the time. After he rang off, I called Peter. He was elated, but as sanguine as ever.

'After that first time in Oslo, you can never be surprised. It's got to come uncorked at some time during the season. But it will have surprised the Finns. After the last two seasons they have been saying he should take a rest. The effect on me is the same as in 1979 – it's good to know we've got this far in the season without too much work. It leaves us room for development, but we'll have to re-examine his racing programme for the next few weeks and see where we can slow down a bit. I definitely want him to ease off. These solo runs where he is out on his own are very draining. When we go for the longer records they will need

142

to be more carefully thought out. You don't get an 'accidental' record over four laps.'

This latest achievement, a record among records, produced a spate of speculation in the press about alleged unique factors in Seb's running. Newspapers 'discovered' aspects of his training and physique of which even he was unaware! Peter was moved to write in *Athletics Weekly* under the headline 'Myth Making With Sebastian Coe':

'There is a myth being spread that Sebastian has a secret training method. In fact, according to Peter Hildreth in the *Sunday Telegraph* it is so good that it saves him from using drugs to beat the world's best and I have a duty to disclose this secret to the coaching world in order to save our youth from the dreaded pills (why not have a simple moral objection?). An alternative 'secret' was disclosed in a strip in the *Sunday Times* which suggests that their illustrated exploits of Seb's rope-climbing, box-bounding, striding and leaping are the reason for his success. Why do I feel so concerned over articles about which it could be said that they only purport to show how great is my athlete? Because they can easily fool young and enthusiastic athletes and, even worse, whether the writers realize it or not, they cast a slur on professional coaches and the BAAB coaching system. I have also seen this rubbish published in American running magazines headed 'Seb's Secret Training'. I think it is worth noting here that I am the *only* coach Sebastian has ever had from the day he first started running. No one else has had any say of any kind in his training, racing programme or in the compilation of a planned career on the country, road or track. If anyone knew of a secret it would be me, and I would have thought that any searcher for the 'great truth' would have asked me and not other people.

Before Seb even saw Loughborough University, I met George Gandy and got his agreement to supervise Seb's circuit and weight training, which George has done carefully and meticulously. That's long-term planning. Seb was never an athlete away from home, lost and looking for advice – that's not my style. A coach should build a back-up team: we have our own favourite and proven physiotherapists at our three working bases, Sheffield, Leicester and London. Physiological advice is available in Leeds and Loughborough. But only *one* coach. No athlete will succeed when listening to too many people. Only one can call the shots.

'Now about motivation. If you are not self-motivated you are wasting your time, and everyone else's. No coach can be giving you his best attention if he has to wonder if you will turn up or carry out his instructions when you are on your own. Instead of working on your improvement, he's wasting his emotional and nervous energy. Emotional? Yes, because he must believe passionately in what he's doing. Not for me the aloof and distant pose. I can't run the races, but by God I'm involved in winning. This search for 'secrets' and 'gimmicks' obscures the fact that there is not any short cut to the top. Not one. Symptomatic of this search for magic was the insulting idea that if we wanted medals in the Olympics and other major Championships we should send our athletes abroad to foreign coaches. East Germany was suggested for example. How on earth did Wells, Thompson, Ovett, Coe, Oakes and our girls ever manage their medal achievements? Are we so conditioned to failure that secretly we need to find excuses for success? Are we really so timid? At world level, athletics is currently our most successful sport, above all others.

'I can give any athlete the recipe for success, but it is not the magic formula. It's only the list of ingredients. They are, in order of importance: Talent (there is no substitute for this), Motivation, Dedication and Loyalty. Loyalty to a coach is very important. Why don't I mention beating a path to the door at Loughborough? Because there isn't anything new there in the gymnasium or weight room. When I showed the *Sunday Times* strip to Seb he laughed and said, "I've been doing it for years, along with 40 to 80 others, some of whom do the exercises better than I do." So it can't be there. Why don't I write down my secret training, sell it, and retire for life, rich, anywhere in the world. For one very good reason and one only . . . it does not exist!

Seb is trained in an orthodox fashion using known methods. A coach, I believe it was Harry Wilson, once said that coaches get a reputation for knowing a lot about athletes, when in reality they know a lot about some athletes. And that is a very large part of coaching: knowing the athlete intimately. Choose a coach carefully, and unless you are totally certain your coach is not the one for you, stick with him. Chopping and changing tells more about you than the coach. His success depends so much on continuity. My success with Seb is only possible through his loyalty to me, wherein I can experiment slowly (only varying one factor at a time) and check my results. I use a basic five-tier training system, which I discussed with Frank Horwill as long ago as 1971:

The way I use 300 metre sessions was influenced by Wilf Paish.
My little knowledge of physiology is enhanced by Dr John Humphreys and others. These people's work is freely available.
When I attended coaching conferences, so did many others, we all drew from the same pool.
I build Seb's programme year by year with the bricks of my training – Frank Dick would call this periodizing – using micro and macro cycles.
The energy systems I seek to develop and use are those explained in the publications of work-physiologists. The duration and intensity of the stimuli is known to many others.

'What is special is only that Seb's training is tailored specifically to him and his requirements by a coach who is in a unique position of being able to have detailed knowledge of his charge. My point is that there are not any magic formulae. A logical, intelligent application of widely-known facts, damned hard work by an athlete and coach alike, no neglected details, meticulous care, dedication . . . these are the requirements. If I bring anything new to coaching, it is what I said in a seminar in America eighteen months ago: think like a good modern industrial manager, identify your short-term and long-term objectives, marshal your resources and co-ordinate your help. Above all think first, and then act with conviction. In the UK all that we require are better facilities and nationally organized sports medicine as a back-up for our coaches.

'Why not for once opt for the simple explanation? Endowed by nature with the right equipment, loyal to one coach (this has given me time to succeed), dedicated to hard training and being totally disciplined, Seb has become, simply, very good at his job. In other words, Sebastian Coe *has made himself* better than the rest. That is the lesson for all to see.'

The week after Florence Seb was due to run for Loughborough at home against the AAA, but went down with a stomach virus and a large crowd was disappointed, unnecessarily because match officials delayed an announcement even when he had already been removed to the University sanitorium. It was an unfortunate incident. Seb also had to withdraw from the international against West Germany and Poland the following week – two days after which Ovett, running in the Bislett Games in Oslo, was beaten in the mile by the young American Tom Bayers, the hare who memorably ran away from the field, in this case never to be caught.

Seb recovered in time to travel to Helsinki with the British team for the Europa Cup semi-final. In a spectacular two-day meeting, with nine victories in twenty events including five on the second day, they beat the Russians for the first time ever. Keith Stock, who was to have a brilliant summer repeatedly raising the UK pole-vault record, epitomized the British effort. For eighteen months he had been voluntarily unemployed in order to train full-time while his wife Debbie worked to pay for his £120 poles. Vaulting into a difficult wind he cleared 18ft 4½ in to beat Brian Hooper's record by half an inch, leaving Russian's Olympic silver medallist Volkov in fourth place. Other stirring victories on the second day came from Allan Wells (200 metres) and Barry Smith (by millimetres in the 5,000 metres), plus Seb in the 800 metres, to add to those of Ovett (1,500 metres), Wells (100 metres) and Roy Mitchell (long-jump) on the first day. Seb led all the way in the 800 metres from the Moscow bronze medallist Kirov, holding off the Russian's challenge on the last bend with a surge which opened a 10-metre gap within 50. In his first race for over three weeks his time of 1:47·57 was almost six seconds outside his world record, yet the final sprint confirmed his recovery – the fastest last 100 ever in an 800 metres with 11·3.

     ❬ There was a fabulous team spirit, and when we all arrived back at the hotel, Bill Evans, the Chairman of the Board, was standing at the main entrance to shake the hand of every member of the team, a marvellous gesture which did not go unnoticed. I felt good after my race and was reasonably optimistic that, given the right weather, I could do something worthwhile in Stockholm. 〉

Two days later, Seb was due to step out amid the echoes of history. In the Olympic Stadium in Stockholm, which has seen fifty-five world records since 1912, he was to attempt to recapture the 1,500 metres record taken from him by Ovett in Koblenz the previous autumn. Back home in Sheffield, just before leaving for Helsinki, he had run his most remarkable sequence yet of 800s in training, faster even than during his preparation for the Olympics.

Three times the 1,500 metres record had fallen in Stockholm, the last time to the legendary Swede, Gunder Hagg, almost forty years before. Seb was aiming to be some 16 seconds faster, indeed to be the first man under 3:30. However, things were to go sadly astray. Upon arrival from Helsinki, it was soon apparent that Heinz Lueger, the promoter, had neither assembled a really strong field nor realized the importance of adequate interval times to be given to the leaders, as is legally permitted. James Robinson of America, second fastest of the year over 800, had been asked to push out the first two laps, but his own judgement of 800 pace was so consistently erratic that it had to be doubted whether he could usefully gauge the pace up to the half-way stage for the four-lap man.

Seb telephoned Peter the night before the race, and agreed that what was required was an 800 in 1:52 followed by a third lap of 57, leaving him needing a last 300 in 42. That would yield 3:31; a sub-41 final 300 would beat the 3:30 barrier. I went for a stroll with Seb late in the evening in one of the city's handsome parks, because he wanted to be sure he slept well, and he admitted that his main aim was to improve on his own best time. The next morning we went on a long boat trip with mothers and school children round the huge harbour and stopped off to visit the National Maritime Museum. The sky was clear, the wind muted, the sun warm: and by the time of the race, on a golden evening, there was not even a zephyr to disturb the flags around the stadium. It was as perfect for record breaking as could be.

❛ Yet in a strange way there was a 'down market' feeling. I'd chosen Stockholm for a 1,500 because I knew I would go for the mile in Zürich and again in Brussels. But things weren't right. Because, in some areas, athletics has become a circus, some promoters get the idea that being *nice* is more important than putting on an efficient meeting. There's too much of a situation in which every athlete runs every meeting, so why should the promoter make special arrangements if the athletes are treating it no differently from the meeting two nights before? What Lueger didn't realize was that I pick specific meetings for specific purposes. For 1981, I laid my season very carefully, and Stockholm was to be my only 1,500 metres. ❜

Disappointingly, Seb squandered his great talent and a perfect evening in a shambles of a race. Robinson ran a suicidal first two laps, the first 400 some four seconds ahead of Ovett's run in Koblenz. Seb was quickly obliged to drop off the front pace, and was left in a vacuum eight metres down on Robinson, but way ahead of the pack including Scott and others. At the 800 mark Seb was almost four seconds ahead of Ovett's schedule, and still more than two seconds up at 1,200, having run wholly alone. Inevitably tiring and fading badly, he dragged himself round the final 300 in a slow 43·6 for an overall 3:31·95, inside his own best, but half a second outside Ovett's.

❛ It was one of the most painful and disappointing races I have run. I might just as well have been out there and run the whole race on my own like a time trial. Throughout, I never received a single lap time. The organizers had said they had prepared everything, but I was running in the dark. I went after Robinson thinking 'he's really motoring'. I was fairly stretched, and there *he* was seven paces clear! I dropped off his pace as far as I dared, but that meant I couldn't hear the times they were calling to him, and they had no one calling them to me. At 1,200 I knew that it had probably been blown, and that from now on it was just a question of trying to remain standing up. I was pretty sick. An athlete only has a few such occasions in his racing life, when he is ready and the weather is right. I had not discussed the race with any of the other runners, because I like to leave that to the

148

organizers, but I was left with the feeling that I had made a huge effort all for nothing. The 1,200 time of 2:48·3, I'm convinced, could be OK but only if arrived at by a different breakdown. What was so ridiculous was the crazy distribution of effort. If the first half of the race had been two seconds slower, I would probably have gone under 3:31. Just to rub salt into the wound, Lueger came bounding across to me at the finish all beams and exclaimed, 'Congratulations, a new stadium record!' But at least when I looked at the video, I was quite pleased that I did manage to hold my rhythm down the finishing straight. **'**

Peter, who had been unable to take time off to travel to Stockholm, was more philosophical – although, in the light of such an exceptional time, he knew better than most just what might have been achieved with more even pace distribution. With the huge crowd still basking in the evening sun, while British typewriters clattered out the news for home consumption, Seb chatted to Peter over the phone. It had been Seb's decision to go for the record, so it was he who now bore a heavier weight of disappointment than his coach, though both sensed instinctively that, had Peter been there, his presence would have provided the critical difference. With American Ben Plucknett, the massive shot-putter, still strutting around the arena following a world record which would evaporate in a drug exposé a few days later, Peter said to me:

'It's not so much a matter of the promoter having put up the pace which went wrong, it was not having someone giving Seb the times which he would understand. You've got to know the splits. If you want a 1:52 and someone goes out and does 1:49, you should have the judgement to stay off the pace, but then you need the confirmation of your own time. I didn't want Seb particularly to go for the record at this stage, but under the pressure of a record attempt anyone has to have that split-second guidance to make adjustments. Mind you, I'm not sure that he was physically one hundred per cent ready for the longer race after the illness.'

Back at the hotel Seb had a massage which eased some of the disappointment, and left him feeling mentally more in tune for a

149

tilt at his own 1,000 metres time in Oslo four days later. He did not pay too much attention to a slight soreness on the outside ball of his right foot just behind the little toe.

Before the start of the season he had been scheduled to run an 800 metres at Bislett, in a meeting at which the main attraction was the Dulux Dream Mile, a label fit to make one's grandfather turn in his grave but now simply another vehicle of the commercial cavalcade which rolls across Europe from June to September. When Arne Haukvik had seen what had happened in Florence, however, he realized that to get a record out of Seb – expediency is fairly flagrant – it would be better if Seb were switched to a 1,000 metres. In three previous appearances at Bislett, Seb had set three records and Haukvik avariciously eyed a fourth.

On arrival at the Panorama Hotel, however, Seb discovered that there was no sort of field at all for the 1,000, and he began to conceive the idea of a switch to the Dream Mile and a confrontation with Ovett. He was willing, but was the other guy? After a relaxing ten mile run around the lake, the suggestion was put to Haukvik's chief assistant, Sven Arne Hansen, who looked like an entrepreneur who had just been asked to get Reagan and Brezhnev together at the same table for a chess match. Just think of the tickets, but think of the hassle! Hansen said with a slightly pale smile that it was a great idea, and he would see what he could do. But a few hours later came back with the answer: allegedly, Andy Norman had said on behalf of Ovett that a promise had been given to the IAAF not to pre-empt their Golden Mile in Brussels – to which both were obviously invited. A check by John Rodda of *The Guardian* yielded a denial by the IAAF, so it became apparent to Seb that he was being frozen out of the race either by Ovett or the organizers. Certainly somebody somewhere did not want the confrontation. If nothing else, the attempt had clearly disclosed to Ovett that Seb was ready and, indeed, eager for a race.

When Peter arrived forty-eight hours beforehand, he immediately set about trying to arrange for more quality to be injected into the 1,000 metres and the best that the Norwegians could come up with was to persuade American 400 metres hurdler James King to run again forty-five minutes after his own speciality. For the second time in five days Seb was blessed with a perfect evening; the tranquillity of Scandinavian summers is something quite unique, and the surroundings of the Panorama Hotel, in undulating grasslands and pinewood at the end of Oslo's picturesque little 'overground' underground railway line, generates a mood which comes close to the ideal for athletes. Peter would say later: 'The poverty of the field which was tossed up served to inspire both of us. For an athlete of his calibre, who always delivers the goods, you'd expect a better field. After being elbowed out of the Dream Mile there was no way he was not going to get the 1,000.' In defence of Haukvik and Hansen, it has to be said it is now difficult to find serious top flight two-lap runners who are eager to race against Seb, because of the inevitability of being made to look slow. It was at this stage that the IAAF issued a warning that records would be invalid if pace-makers dropped out.

King, in all-red, went off at a crisp pace, with Rob Harrison of Liverpool Harriers dropping in behind Seb in third place after 200 metres, having generously agreed to take it up from 400 to 600. Peter had planned a 400 in 52·5, an 800 in 1:45. Now the bustling King reached the 400 in 51, Harrison sustained it to 600 in a ferocious 78, and Seb launched out for home, passing the 800 in 1:44·4, which was inside the time in which Robinson had shortly beforehand won the individual 800. Peter, on the inside of the track, said to himself 'it's in the bag'.

❡ For the first time ever in a race I was aware of the clock as I came into the finishing straight off the final bend. With 50 yards or so to go I could see it winking alongside the photo-finish camera, '2:5, 2:6 . . . ' The clock was going faster and I was going slower. I began to feel my right leg packing up, losing drive, for some reason. My head was so far back that it felt it was almost touching my spine. If I had been a walker, I'd have been done for lifting! It seemed that my feet were only barely leaving the ground. It was the toughest of all my records. ❡

The fourth 200 had been covered in 26·2, the last 200 in 27·6, and Seb had brought his record down by more than a second to 2:12·18. It was that fourth half-lap, after he took over from Harrison, which had bust the record – over a second faster than the same stage a year before. On television Coleman was yelling 'this must be the greatest front runner of all time'. Peter, as usual, was delighted but still earthbound.

'It would have been faster but for Stockholm. But aggro doesn't slow him up, just the reverse. The 1,000 is the cruellest race on the track. Seb has turned the 800 into a sprint, but to run 1:45 and then carry on another half-lap is something special. It's that ability which prevented him being run out by Straub in Moscow. Pace judgement is vital. If you get any of the first 800 wrong you will cave in over the last 200. A final 200 of 27·0 is not outstanding in a mile, but coming after an 800 it is fantastic. The 1,000 doesn't have the glamour, but just look at the milers who can't manage it, such as Cram and Maree.'

In the clamour of the press conference afterwards, with journalists from all over Europe, Seb was immediately asked what were his main engagements for the rest of the season, and replied that they would be a mile in Zürich, followed by his Golden Mile in Brussels, and finally the 800 metres in the World Cup in Rome. The invitations for Brussels had already gone out and Seb, only a day or two previously, had been among the first to make a firm acceptance. Peter had told the British Board, and also Andy Norman, that whether or not Ovett chose to be there, Seb *would* be, come what may. Thus the tension and expectation in the packed little Bislett bowl on that July evening after Seb's record was now intense as we awaited the Dream Mile. Earlier in the week Ovett, within twenty-four hours of Seb's 1,500 metres run in Stockholm, had produced an identical time of 3:31·95 in Milan. Would he now, in his fourth record bid of the season, improve on the mile he had taken from Seb here a year ago?

As usual Bob Benn led through the first two laps, in 1:55, and then let Ovett and the rest through on the inside – though, as King did in the 1,000, he was careful to finish the race to comply with the new IAAF directive. Byers, who had run away from everyone fifteen days before, now took over the third lap, but was passed just before the bell by Scott and Ovett (2:53·5). Scott held on until the pack, still eight strong, swept into the final bend. Thomas Wessinghage made a brief challenge, but Ovett kicked clear, followed by Walker and Scott. Ovett looked in supreme shape as he headed for the tape, and behind him one of the greatest finishes ever seen was taking place. By a fraction Ovett was outside his own 3:48·68, but was still the third fastest ever with 3:49·25. Other records tumbled. José Luis Gonzalez burst through for second, and a Spanish best of 3:49·67; Scott's 3:49·68 at last lowered Ryun's fourteen-year-old American record. Walker in fourth place had his second best ever of 3:50·26; American Todd Harbour had 3:50·34; and the remarkable young Cram clipped more than three seconds off his best for 3:50·38. Wessinghage was on 3:50·91, and John Robson was a 'mere' eighth in a personal best of 3:52·34. As that great campaigner Walker said: 'That has to be the greatest mile race of all. At my age I should know. I seem to have run in most of them over the last few years.' Inevitably, almost before Ovett had crossed the line, he was asked if he would now be in Brussels, and said he would. 'If Seb is there, then there is going to be a race.'

What he didn't know at that moment was that a major problem had overtaken Seb. The blister which had formed in Stockholm had now burst, slicing off a thick lump of hardened skin on the point of maximum pressure. He would have to withdraw from a race in Dublin the following week, and all track-work in training would have to be suspended. For how long?

11: See-saw Summit

6 This was the most frustrating part of the season. I returned home, had the foot well strapped, and for the next few days went for gentle runs on grass. Peter's view was that, with five-and-a-half weeks to Zürich, I should do little or nothing for the next three weeks other than just tick over up in the hills. That's the great advantage of having someone there in the background who is not involved hour by hour, who can stand back and say, 'forget it, drop down three or four pegs, and then go back up again. You'll never hold a peak for five-and-a-half weeks anyway, and then another two-and-a-half to Rome.' I probably bridled a bit. My experience would have told me that it was what I needed to do, but I didn't know whether I had the mental discipline to carry it out. It doesn't matter how experienced an athlete is, we're all too close to what we're doing, too introspective, always to know what's best. A week lost at the wrong time can set you back, but a week off at the right time can be beneficial.

The vital thing about a good coach is that he should *know*. It's easy to prescribe extra work, but it takes a lot of conviction to say 'stop'. This has been Peter's strength. He's always had the ability, during a training session, to say 'right, that's it, I've seen enough'. So few coaches are sufficiently sure of themselves to know when to stop. So now I kept in shape by easy running in the Peaks, by going to the gym for body-work, by doing a few 'strides', but keeping off the track and giving the skin a chance to reform. After a couple of weeks the English summer had turned so miserable that we decided to go elsewhere for some sun. I was reduced to running in Sheffield in a water-proof track-suit in July! After a couple of easy domestic races I flew off to Nice for rest and recuperation. 9

Peter was pragmatic. 'Although I always like to plan for the major events at the end of the season, Seb tends to blow his cork early, to be ready too soon, but on the whole it doesn't tend to worry us because at that stage we haven't done too much speed work. But, as Seb says, showing restraint when you are doing well is difficult for both coach and athlete.' Perhaps Seb had a shade too much rest in Nice – at any rate he returned home and ran, for him, like a zombie in the Talbot Games 800 metres.

❝ It was the closest I came to losing a race all year. I was mentally refreshed, had a nice sun-tan, but was too relaxed. It made me think of the motto of that great Norwegian runner of the fifties, Auden Boysen, who used to say 'brown legs never run fast', that too much sun does you no good. At the bell I was down on James King, but comfortable. In the back straight I started to wind it up, but suddenly found Gary Cook going past me and was nearly boxed by Dave Warren. Shades of Moscow! I managed to react just in time and overhaul Gary in the final straight. Yet I wasn't surprised that Gary should run me close, because earlier in the week he'd had a personal best of 1:45·42 in beating Boit and Schmid in Budapest. ❞

Talbot staged an exciting Games, with American Mel Lattany setting a UK all-comers record of 10·6 for the 100 metres, against Wells's 10·15 at Meadowbank in 1978. Ovett, having fitted in a 3:49·66 mile in Lausanne and then a 3:31·57 over 1,500 in Budapest, was now hard pressed in a 1,000 metres by Steve Cram, getting home in a relatively slow 2:20·67.

Doubt had already crept in about the confrontation with Seb which the sporting world was awaiting in Brussels. The AAA had organized a minor international in Norway and it was being said that Ovett's obligation would lie there, 'with his country'. The AAA, in the confused administration of British athletics, is the body which sanctions overseas races for individuals, and Seb had had to tell them firmly that he had no intention of backing down on his acceptance to Brussels. The story took a further twist a few days after the Talbot Games, when Ovett tore a calf muscle in training, had to pull out of the AAA Championships the following weekend, and also missed the Europa Cup Final in Zagreb.

Seb was aiming for his first AAA senior title in the 800 metres. With some crazily uneven seeding for the heats, he had to run close to the championship record to qualify on the Friday evening, while Rob Harrison blew up at 600 and was eliminated. The following day I drove to Crystal Palace with Seb for the final, and there was an unusual illustration of his capacity for shutting off mentally before an important race when, in heavy traffic and in danger of being late to begin warming up, he slept soundly in the passenger seat over the last five miles to the stadium.

❦ It was the fastest anyone had ever had to run in the heats to qualify – 1:45·8. The seeding showed some alarming ineptitude. The slowest heat was 1:51, and the imbalance allowed some average foreign talent to get through to the final at the expense of promising British runners, who deserved the exposure and experience of running in their own national championships. In the final I'd made a mental note not to lose concentration as I had in the Talbot, and I started winding it up hard off the penultimate bend. There was a good run by young Chris McGeorge in third place behind Omar Khalifa, my colleague at Loughborough from Sudan. But soon after the finish I found I was in serious trouble. When I took off my right shoe I found blood coming through the sock. The new skin on the blister from Oslo had ruptured, and this time it was right through to the flesh which was cracked and bleeding. I knew in an instant that all the plans and ambitions for the climax to the season were jeopardized, that my season could be ended there and then. ❦

It was not a pretty sight. As Dr Archibald, consultant surgeon at The West Middlesex Hospital, cut away more dead skin in the medical room beneath the stadium, anxiously watched by Peter, the total raw area was now almost as big as a two pence piece. From my own experience in football I knew that such an injury would have difficulty healing again in a short space of time – and the Europa Final was only eight days away. Even if Seb managed to run in that, it could finish him completely for Zürich and Brussels. It was a risk he knew there was no avoiding.

❝ If it was the last time I was able to stand up that summer, I just had to be there in Zagreb with the British team for the final. I had to accept that I would have to sacrifice my own aims if necessary, because I could not possibly opt out of Zagreb, and then turn up to run for myself in Zürich and Brussels. Obviously I would not be able to train properly in the week ahead on the speed sessions I had planned – as much in preparation for the mile in Zürich as the 800 metres in Zagreb.

Dr Archibald's frank opinion was that I ought not to run again for the rest of the season, yet I had no choice and, in spite of knowing that the track in Zagreb in August could be hot enough to fry an egg, Sunday's 800 was part of the work I ought to be doing in the next week to bring me to a peak for Zürich. It was a daunting thought, and I admit I felt a bit depressed as I went jogging the next morning in West London, with the foot heavily strapped, before flying off to the Swiss mountains at Macolin where I was due at the national training school to join Mike Boit and Tom Byers. I received some marvellous treatment on the way from a Swiss doctor in Zürich, who gave me a protective layer of plastic skin and made sure there was no infection. Even so, the foot was still sore and I had to wind down again, managing only one track session of some 300s with Mike before I flew on to Zagreb. When I'd arrived at Macolin he could hardly move. For a spot of diversion the previous day, he had run up the two mile concrete slope alongside the funicular railway which climbs up to Macolin from the town of Biel – a gradient of about 1 in 3! My foot was healing well, although it was still tender. As I had feared, it was baking hot when I joined the British team in Zagreb, and I realized that it was going to be in the balance getting through Sunday's race without any set-back and further damage. ❞

There was a sharp difference of opinion on how Seb should strap his foot for the race. Peter, who would not be there, had favoured a lint dressing underneath an adhesive bandage. But just before leaving London, Seb had bumped into Eddie Franklin, Chelsea's physiotherapist, who recommended that he should strap the elastoplast directly onto the wound, so that it would adhere to the thin film of new skin and there would be no friction, the plaster itself acting as a skin. Peter had painstakingly applied plastic skin but this was still highly vulnerable.

6 A large number of British supporters had gone to Zagreb for the final, some had taken holidays in caravans and were on a site immediately beside the training track, giving us cups of tea and coffee and Coke after we had finished. It was a pleasant atmosphere, but as with all the three European Finals in which I have run, the mood among the team lacked the edge and determination that had been there for the semi-finals. Some of the team were too relaxed, as if they considered that the hard bit had already been done, rather than that it was still to come. There was not the same sense of urgency now that there had been in Helsinki, and the first day was a bit disappointing. Then Mark Holthom opened the second day with a fine win in the high hurdles; Julian Goater ran a really intelligent, cagey race to take second in the 10,000 metres ahead of Fleschen of East Germany; and Dave Moorcroft, in spite of injuries, ran a tremendously gutsy 5,000 metres to beat a strong field. I had mixed feelings: whenever I run an 800 metres now in an international I feel under pressure because of Moscow. I get the feeling, from ordinary people as well as from television commentators and some of the press, that I will never be able to win often enough to live that down. 9

Under the pressure of needing every point in their battle to finish ahead of Russia, East Germany were using cloak and dagger tactics over who would run for them in the 800 metres. On the first day Beyer had won the 1,500 metres. Steve Cram, running well outside his potential, was beaten into third place. Wagenknecht was listed to run the 800 metres, but rumour had it that Beyer would replace him at the last minute. The British team managers could get no confirmation, so an hour before the race I went off to where the East Germans had their warm-up group – in the shade! – hoping to discover the answer. Both runners appeared to be limbering up, but when Wagenknecht broke away from the group I was able to approach him and ask what was going on. 'Beyer will run' he told me, clearly annoyed by the decision. I informed Seb, who was relieved to know what he had to beat. Following a fast time in his national championships, Beyer had been claiming, I felt optimistically, that he was capable of approaching Seb's world record before the end of the season.

Seb answered the doubters with a clean tactical race, repeating his 1979 victory in Turin. He took the lead towards the end of the first back straight and went through the bell with Zivotic in 54·81, Wulbeck bringing up the rear. Round the final bend Wulbeck, having come through powerfully, and Beyer made a challenge, only for Seb to accelerate clear and win by five or six strides as the two Germans beat the air in vain behind him. The race had been conveniently slow under a scorching sun, and the foot came through unscatched. Peter would have to accept, grudgingly, that Franklin's soccer remedy, in the event, protected the forthcoming climax to the whole summer.

❛ I was lucky no one wanted to make the pace, so that we had a soft first lap and I was in a position to dictate from the front fairly comfortably coming off the third bend. The foot was sore, but no further damage had been done.

It was a thrilling run later on by Dave Moorcroft, even if Barry Smith didn't deserve to be dropped after winning the semi-final. With Aston Moore coming second in the triple jump, and the 400 metres relay boys getting third, we took an overall third place behind East Germany and Russia for the first time ever, finishing nine-and-a-half points ahead of West Germany. They spend a fortune on athletics and there were some pretty serious post-mortems, I hear. It was a real blow to their prestige. ❜

Back in Zürich for the simultaneous attempt on the 1,500 metres and mile, Seb stayed out of town to try and avoid the pressure he had inevitably placed on himself by making the intent known well in advance. A twelve-strong field, including almost everyone of note other than Ovett and Coghlan, had been assembled by Andreas Brugger, the promoter. A problem arose on the afternoon of the race, however, when Tom Byers, who had recently run a 1,000 metres in an outstanding 2:16, found he was having some trouble with his breathing, the legacy of a heavy cold. Not only this, but his coach Pete Petersen was expressing serious doubts about Seb's request for a first 1,200 in around 2:49. 'I just don't think anyone can do that and still keep going for the fourth lap on schedule.' At that stage he still had to have final discussions with Peter about the pace.

❮ I accept that I put pressure on myself over the weeks beforehand, but when the day arrived the tension down in the hotel near the stadium was incredible. I'd come in from out of town, and as I checked in to my room there really was that feeling of the sky pressing down, of the walls crowding in on me – the kind of expectancy there is said to be a few hours before a world heavy-weight-title fight. The sheer dimension of the meeting adds to the fascination of the mood beforehand, with over a hundred of the world's top athletes all there together, the biggest event outside the Olympics or the European Championships. Brugger stages the best invitation meeting in the world, and once you do this, then the expectation of the crowd keeps pace with the glamour, they want something better with each succeeding year. What really wound me up as taut as a violin string was when a BBC television director said to me on the day of the race: 'You do realize we're breaking into the 'Nine O'Clock News' for this, it's pretty important it comes off.'' Suddenly you realize the extent to which you have set yourself up in front of millions of people back home. A remark like that suddenly puts a ton on your shoulders, though I don't mean to be critical, because I realize the value to the sport that such TV exposure gives in one of the main pro-grammes of the day. I think it's an honour that a race should be thought to be of such interest. ❯

The race plan, the only one to which Seb has ever been a carefully involved party, was for Byers to take it to 1,000 metres and then for Boit to pick it up for as long as he could thereafter. Byers's cold now posed a serious question mark, while Boit was doubtful about his ability to get to the front at the stage and at the speed which would be required. 'I'm not used to these longer races.' In the dim half-darkness of the warm-up area, a football pitch adjacent to the stadium, the collection of great runners began circling, separately, introspectively, like sea-gulls circling before a storm. Occasionally two of them would pause and merge, then go their separate ways off into the darkness again. Walker was grimly purposeful: the big New Zealander has a strong inner pride, and although he has stretched his time at the top past its natural limit, he meant this race to be his as much as anyone else's.

The blond Scott, still with the air of a college boy though he had become a father for the first time a few days beforehand, seemed relaxed. Cram, conscious that he had squandered the chance to win an important cup race in Zagreb, quietly stretched his hamstrings, using the rail around the pitch like a ballet dancer. I told him, for what it was worth, that I thought Scott would be chiefly watching his American rival Harbour. Wessinghage went padding by with his athlete wife a stride behind, a common sight on the athletic scene. Seb seemed tense and preoccupied, his shoulders hunched the way they usually are when he is not relaxed. A bevy of tiny autograph hunters kept infiltrating onto the pitch, getting in the way like sheep on a railway track, scurrying out from under his feet as he floated past, oblivious. Peter chatted on the rail with Petersen, physicists at the countdown, checking their data.

From inside the stadium a sustained roar from the 25,000 crowd pursued Coghlan and the local hero Ryffel round the final lap of a thrilling 5,000 metres, the Irishman nosing in front for a stadium record in 13:19·13. Seb, looking up at the sky, held out the palms of his hands as though he had felt rain, but there was nothing there. The moment had come. There was a precedent to beat: Renaldo Nehemiah had earlier set a breath-taking world record of 12·93 in the high hurdles. Seb's edginess continued when he was there on the track, waiting, with the 200 metres event still to be run. As the twelve went to the line, the conditions were once more perfect. Byers towed them through the first lap in 56·1 with Seb in second place, Gonzalez and Boit following. Now Byers involuntarily let the pace slacken fractionally for a second lap of 57·5 and a half way time of 1:53·6 – outside the 1:53 Seb had wanted, but ahead of Ovett's schedule at the same time in Oslo the year before. Boit and Cram were tucked in close behind. Coming off the bend Byers's head began to roll.

❝ I realized Tom was fading, but wondered for another 100 yards or so whether he might pick it up again, and I wondered, too, whether Mike would come through. By the time I realized Tom had nothing left, we were down the back straight and almost into the bend. I knew I had to go, but that hesitation for 70 or 80 yards had cost me at least a second – and I felt too good for that stage. ❞

Boit made no bid, just hanging on, and when Seb reached the bell, a 58·0 third lap made the 1,200 yards time 2:51·7, almost a second outside Ovett's in Oslo. The chance of the 1,500 record had almost certainly gone and Seb was going to have to dig hard to take even the mile. Straining down the back straight, he opened a gap on Boit and Cram, but the 1,500 metres went by in 3:33·3, almost two seconds outside the record and half a second down on Ovett at the same stage. Yet now Seb found an uplifting surge to claw back one half of his objective, crossing the line in 3:48·53 to clip 0·27 off the mile record.

     6 In theory, 3:33 at 1,500 meant that the mile record was lost, because when I first broke the record in 1979 with 3:49 I'd done 3:32·8 at 1,500. The way we'd planned to treat the race was as a hard 1,500, hoping to maintain form over another 109 metres. The way it worked out, the last part was the hardest, and it's fortunate that I had improved my finishing speed. 9

Ovett's final 109 metres in Oslo had been 16·1; Seb's was 15·3. Behind him the thirty-four-year-old Boit set an African record 3:49·74, while Cram, already the world's fastest twenty-year-old, improved to an astonishing 3:49·95 in third place. Walker, finishing faster than anyone, said with irritation: 'I had far too much left.' Scott, tired from his trans-Atlantic flight, could finish only eighth. The scene after the finish was an extraordinary anomaly, with celebration up in the stands and despondency down on the track. Seb loped off down the back straight, head down, staring at the track, deaf to the applause. From 200 yards away his disappointment in himself was clearly evident. Up in the main tribune Brugger, scarlet-blazered, was busy acknowledging the acclaim like some Roman emperor. Angela Coe, who had hardly dared watch, was for a few seconds unclear whether either record had gone or not, more sensitive than anyone to that lonely picture of disappointment moving slowly down the far side of the stadium. Byers, too, was dejected, feeling he had let Seb down and apologized to Peter. 'What!' said Peter, 'was the record broken or not?' His compassion was all for the young American.

❛ I felt mentally done in. I'd lived ten days with the worry of the blister and the thought that it could be the last chance of a record that year, because Brussels would have to be first and foremost a race. I'd missed the 1,500, and didn't believe I'd done enough to protect the mile record for even the rest of the season, and was proved right a week later. ❜ .

Not the least of Peter's qualities is his equanimity. Occasionally touchy, sometimes belligerent when wanting to make a point, he views every race as a positive experience to be utilized in looking ahead to the next, and would not allow Seb to dwell on the paradox of being dissatisfied with the world record.

'Without the problem of the foot, he might have been a little more sure and settled. He wanted a definitive performance, and afterwards he felt, as I did, that the record still wasn't tight. Yet there are not many as tough as he is, it's difficult to run with that kind of blister without favouring the other foot, which in turn can set up muscle problems. I still thought that both records should be obtainable in the same race, yet that third quarter will always be a problem. There's nobody in the world who doesn't think at present that 2:48 is too fast for 1,200, but we reckon it's possible. We may in future look for longer endurance sessions, training repetitions of more than 800. All we knew now was that there were nine days to get right for Brussels. I wasn't as disappointed as Seb was, I knew he could only be better the following week.'

❛ The next morning I went for a brisk seven miles before breakfast, and the countdown to the Golden Mile was as follows:

Friday: home to Sheffield via Manchester, a warm up in the afternoon followed by five half-miles in under two minutes with ninety-second intervals.

Saturday: morning – nine miles cross-country; afternoon – four times 300 in around 36·5 with two-minute recoveries.

Sunday: morning – six times 200 in around 22·5; afternoon – ten times 100 concentrating on 'kick'.

163

Monday: morning – ten miles on the road.

Tuesday: morning – fifteen times 200 in 28·0 with half-minute recovery; afternoon – nine miles through the woods.

Wednesday: morning – fast five miles; afternoon – ten accelerations on hill climbs, followed by four miles.

Thursday: rest day and travel to race.

Friday: morning – twenty-five minutes jogging and strides.

The foot improved considerably and, looking back, I have to concede that the season was blessed with a lot of luck – that where I had bad luck in the shape of injuries I managed to get by, and that on all the important days the weather was favourable. ❡

While Seb was tuning up at home, Ovett and others were descending on Koblenz – though objectives seemed, on the surface, to be confused. The main race of the meeting was scheduled to be a 1,500 metres, yet powerful rumour, well founded, suggested that Ovett wished to make a fresh bid for the mile. As the man who had set the 1,500 record on the new Koblenz track the year before, the organizers were unlikely to deny him, but Wessinghage was adamant that *he* would not run a mile. Other runners, arriving in ones and twos the evening beforehand, could not get a straight answer on what was happening, while Ovett himself stated enigmatically: 'I'll run whatever the promoter wants me to run.' It was not a long shot to guess that the promoter's wishes would not be far from Ovett's, though Freddie Schaeffer, the man in question, hedged. 'I don't know what will happen. Wessinghage doesn't want to run a mile, he says Ovett won't come here to help him in a 5,000. Maybe we shall have two races.' Two races it proved to be – though an hour beforehand, after the meeting had already begun, Byers and Scott had still not been told in which race they would run.

Repeated requests by Pete Petersen had failed to disclose the field for either race. Scott had been asked if he would take the third lap of the mile with Ovett. 'I've told them what they can do with it' he said with a grin, lounging on the grass at one end of the stadium. Eventually he was placed in the 1,500 and, running immediately prior to the mile, produced the fourth fastest time ever of 3:31·96 to beat Wessinghage and Boit, plus Ryun's fourteen-year-old American record of 3:31·1. Such was the confusion at the meeting that, as the milers gathered on the track a few minutes later, officials were frantically measuring and drawing a start line with chalk because none existed. Bob Benn, dutiful as ever, led his friend through the first half mile in 1:53·6, identical to Byers's time in Zürich. James Robinson took over for the next 300, then Ovett moved ahead before the bell, needing a last lap of just under 58 to retrieve the record, and he made it by thirteen hundredths with 3:48·40. There was much speculation that, because the mile had not been in the official programme, the record would not be ratified by the IAAF, but some months later it was.

⟨ I saw the result come up on the news; I'd been pretty certain that Steve would do it, so losing the record was not a shock. Steve had nicked it back, but not by very much, and sitting at home it undoubtedly gave me a bit of impetus, particularly as I knew I was in better shape than the week before. Peter had been busy conditioning me saying, 'the more you want something, the further it goes away'. My best runs have usually come in situations where I have been relaxed in the days beforehand, and Brussels was like that. When I woke on the morning of the race I felt different from Zürich, there wasn't the tension, possibly because I knew that winning the race itself would be a satisfaction. It was like Moscow before the 1,500 metres, I was actually looking forward to the race, although there could have been a snag beforehand.

It was scheduled for 9.20 p.m., but at 8.30 p.m. the meeting was already running twenty minutes late. At 8.45 p.m. I was sitting with Peter, thinking there was still an hour to go, when suddenly they announced that the 200 metres and mile were being switched to bring everything back on schedule. Another quarter of an hour and I would have been caught out badly on the warm-up, not so much physically, as it was a warm night, but mentally. That last half-hour before the race has to have the right pattern.

Just before the start, out in the middle of the track as we were removing our track-suits, Omar Khalifa suddenly produced a post-card from Steve Mitchell, a friend from Loughborough, which he had forgotten to give me in Zürich, picturing an old guy in working clothes with the caption 'OK Coe, the recession's over, come home'. Some people think you're just having a good time abroad! **❯**

Tom Byers had fully recovered from his cold and was now determined to make up for what he still regarded as his lapse in Zürich. 'I really do want to help the fellow. If he wants 2:49 for the three-quarter mark, then he can have it. I won't fade after the first 1,000.' After his American record in Koblenz, Scott was on cloud nine, and was busy telling anyone prepared to listen that he was now 'ready to take Coe'. The ever-smiling Boit was merely going to get in there and do what he could; the growing feeling was that this cunning old racer was using Seb to pace him to his best-ever times rather than the other way round. As the runners were presented to the near fifty thousand crowd, the atmosphere was alive with a special hum. The *Daily Mail* may have warned that morning, 'anyone who goes in there tonight other than to win the race may get surprised', but there was no avoiding the question on everyone's mind: would the record change hands for the third time in nine days?

The runners went to the line, Boit, Byers, Coe, Coghlan, Flynn, Khalifa, Masback, Maree, Robson, Scott, Walker, and Wessinghage. Sydney Maree was the new threat to the established men, a black South African who had just acquired American citizenship. At twenty-five, against a background of political controversy, he was thought to be approaching the peak of his career. As the starter got them under orders Seb, in a red Hallamshire vest, was last into line, casually scratching his nose and looking totally relaxed as he leaned forward to await the gun.

There was a lot of bumping and barging on the first bend, Byers immediately leading from Coe, Boit and Coghlan, with Robson lying fifth, Scott badly trapped back in seventh place and Maree bringing up the rear. At the end of the first lap there was a four-yard gap between the front three and the other nine, Byers going through in 54·9, as good as his word.

❮ Immediately into the race I felt good, the very fact that I was running fundamentally for a victory rather than a time producing a better distribution of effort. I followed Tom, able to relax mentally but aware of Mike running slightly wide just behind me. As we entered the second lap I was not consciously thinking of the record, or in any way calculating whether it was 'on'. 〟

Down the back straight for the second time Scott was frantically trying to haul himself back into contention. As the runners went into the fourth bend, Byers's long hair flapping behind him almost in Seb's face, they sped past Peter, a lonely figure sitting on a bench at the 200/600/1000 mark. As Byers, Coe and Boit came off the bend they were fifteen yards up on the rest: clearly something was happening out there, considering the quality of the field, and sure enough Byers went through the half-way mark in 1:52·8, with Seb a fraction down on that in the fastest first half-mile ever run. Into the fifth bend the three figures went, like climbers linked by rope – Byers, the tall, long-striding American, Seb, with almost no rise and fall in his head and shoulders, Boit with his slightly rolling arm and shoulder movement. Coming out of the bend into the back straight, now over a second ahead of Ovett's schedule, there was a near disaster.

〞 I clattered into the back of Byers. It was my fault, I must have momentarily lost concentration. I didn't feel I was going to fall, but the margin must have been very small. I was now aware of the surge of excitement in the crowd, and I was getting the same sensation from the way Peter was shouting the splits. At 1,000 he simply yelled 'yes' and I knew that meant something good. I went past Tom into the bottom bend thinking 'anyone who is going to stay with me now is going to find that it hurts'. 〟

As they came to the bell in 2:51·9, once again outside what Seb would have wished, Boit was hanging on three strides down. Seb needed a last lap of 56·5, for he was now almost half a second outside Ovett's equivalent. But – and this was important – he had the remarkable veteran still pushing him from behind. The television commentators were stressing heavily that Seb was 'behind schedule' and that Boit was threatening. Yet looking at the two runners, there was no comparison. Boit was working hard, Seb was extraordinarily relaxed. The difference between this and all his other major four-lap runs, other than the 1979 Golden Mile, was the smoothness of that last lap. Personally, I was so sure from looking at him that he would be comfortably inside the record that, rather than agonizingly glancing at the clock, I found myself with my eyes exclusively on the runner as the power flowed out of him. Down the back straight the gap was four yards, into the bend it was five, and there was still a glorious kick for home to come, the final margin being almost fifteen yards as Seb stopped the clock at 3:47·33.

6 Mentally, I was actually easing down the fourth back straight. During the race, and again watching the video, I knew I could have been giving it more if I had not been thinking chiefly of winning the race, of saving something for the last 100. If I'd really let go at the bell, I think 3:46·6 was possible that night. Instead, I still had a kick coming off the last bend and my final 100 was better than in any previous four-lap race other than the Olympic Final. But I can't over-estimate the benefit I derived from being pushed from behind by Mike over the last lap, who again lowered the African record with his 3:49·45. My elation at the finish, I admit, was not only due to having got the record back but to having done it in a race, plus the sense of relief that the season was almost over. Yet I still don't think that the mile has been fully tapped. More time will come out of it by running more courageously at the start rather than at the finish. 9

It was his third mile world record in three races, his fourth world record of the summer, his eighth in all, excluding the indoor 800 metres record, and the most achieved by any British athlete ever. Peter, perhaps pardonably, could scarcely contain himself when a microphone was thrust in front of him on the track-side. Had he thought Seb would regain the record? 'I'm human like anyone else, and while I'm overjoyed for him, I'm as smug as anything for myself. So many people were telling me beforehand that the splits were too fast, too ambitious, but they were right on. It was as sweet as anything, and I knew he was going to do it.' The *Sunday Times* commented:

'It would be difficult in future for either Coe's father and coach Peter, or Ovett's right-hand man Andy Norman, to wave away the significance of lost records when both were such excitedly animated figures on the infield of the respective races in Brussels and Koblenz last week. Ovett and Coe were not just trying to win mile races, nor even simply set a world record. They were trying to run faster than the other guy which also happened to mean a world record. And for a brief moment after Coe's race on Friday night, when he turned and gestured towards the stand with his jaw set fast, there seemed an uncharacteristic venom in his expression.'

In the *Observer,* Chris Brasher argued:

'Comparing Coe's new mile record with Ovett's 1,500 metres record, we discover that on Friday night Seb would have been ten-and-a-half yards behind Steve at the 1,500 mark, yet another 119 yards farther on, the added distance for the English mile, Seb would have been eight-and-a-quarter yards ahead of Steve over the mile in Koblenz two nights earlier. That is not the way to bring records down until they are out of reach. To do that Seb needs the presence of Steve – or vice versa. And then we might see a mile in 3:44·3.'

It was through no lack of willingness on Seb's part that such a race did not materialize in the summer of 1981 – though the summer did bring one reward. Both runners received the MBE in the New Year's Honours – but it seemed slightly ludicrous that fellow Olympic gold medallists Allan Wells and Daley Thompson were ignored, Wells having had another superb international season. Seb was also made an Honorary Fellow of Yale University, delivering a lecture on 'Politics and Sport' in February, at a time when his training was interrupted for three weeks by a stress fracture.

12: A New Deal

After the climax of Brussels, Seb's final outing of the summer in the World Cup 800 metres would be a Roman holiday. Or would it? The dark horse was a six-foot two-inch eighteen-year-old Brazilian named Joaquim Cruz, who had been credited with the third fastest time of the year, and of course there was James Robinson. In the event the race was a severe anti-climax, Seb toying with the field to win in 1:46·18. Ovett, meanwhile, was having a relatively harder time in winning the 1,500. The most memorable aspect of the meeting, apart from the all-round failure of the American men, was the sprinting of Evelyn Ashford, and a UK record of 11·10 by Kathy Smallwood in second place in the women's 100 metres.

⁶ If there was ever a chance to put Moscow behind me, this was it. To have lost would have been a blemish on the season, and you are, up to a point, only as good as your last race. I thought it was going to be hard, that I would have to run under 1:44. Mentally I was geared to run till I dropped and, of course, I'm continually fuelled by David Coleman's comments that I'm tactically naïve, and by other people's reactions to him. My error in the Talbot Games put him back on the topic and, according to David, I was in 'all sorts of problems' after only forty metres in Rome. But by 200 it was OK!

At the end of month I went to Baden Baden as a guest of the International Olympic Committee for their congress. I thought I was going for a nice quiet week in a beautiful spa town in the Rhine valley, but it turned out to be almost harder than training. I was made chairman of the athletes and coaches attending the congress, with the job of co-ordinating our contribution and making the best use of the strictly limited times we were given for speaking on the main issues – eligibility/professionalism, doping, female participation on the IOC, politics in sport, and ceremonies (anthems, medals, flags and so on). I had to give the final speech for our group, and we asked the IOC to implement the following actions: a life ban for athletes found to have taken drugs, for coaches who work with or administer drugs, and for doctors who do likewise. Strict penalties for national federations whose athletes or officials are found guilty. More detailed attention to the social care of athletes who make huge sacrifices – academic, social, and in their career – to advance the Olympic movement. The setting up of a permanent Competitors' Commission to provide a link with the IOC and to go alongside the Medical and other Commissions as an advisory group.

We got what we wanted. We will have a Commission, meeting three or four days a year, up until 1984. None of the athletes or coaches there wanted to see the Olympics fade or die, but if the Olympic charter is about fairness in sport, what could be more unfair than the social disregard of the competitors, some of whom can dedicate twelve or thirteen years of their life to the Olympic movement. By social care we mean, of course, the financial regulations. Competitors don't want to be millionaires, but retirement for the average sportsman who has committed himself full-time can be quite traumatic. The IOC should be concerned that everyone comes within their eligibility rule, but it should be left to the federation of each sport to determine what are the needs, financially, within its sport. **9**

The International Amateur Athletic Federation, at its meeting before the start of the World Cup in Rome, went a large part of the way towards admitting a degree of professionalism. It was agreed that athletes would be able to advertise and accept commercial endorsements, provided that the contracts were sanctioned by the national federation, which would retain a percentage of such income for the development of the sport. It will be a matter for negotiation between each athlete and his/her federation as to what this percentage is. What still has to be thrashed out is how much of such 'professional' income may be paid back to the athlete immediately as expenses for training, travelling and subsistence or even vocational training, and how much should be retained 'in trust' until the athlete retires. This is the main area of contention, though the British are among the foremost in recognizing that concessions have to be made if the sport is not to be taken over wholesale. Seb accepts that athletes all have different levels of application as well as ability, and this is why he favours Open, rather than Professional athletics.

❝ At the moment I also feel an element of responsibility in not getting out of athletics too soon. It's in a state of flux, I've never seen a sport so set up for destruction. We must not let it be handed over to the sharks, they're going to have to fight for it. I'm chairman of an off-shoot of the International Athletes Club whose aim is to try to help rationalize Open athletics when it comes, which it must.

I personally would never become a seven-day-a-week professional, because I would never wish to be under contract to anybody or be obliged to run. I would not want to sacrifice my freedom of action, my independence. But for a world-class athlete some of the rules and regulations on expenses are unnecessarily harsh in the costly world of today. Although I don't want a Packer-type circus, which would be crippling for the present framework of international athletics, I think there should be financial flexibility. I've never been able to see why, if you have a talent and you live in a free society, and there is a market for your talent, you should not be allowed to capitalize on it. However much sporting academics and history buffs talk about the evils of abolishing amateurism – and they are mostly over sixty! – when you get down to it, you cannot *eat* goodwill, you cannot get to the top in international sport today without financial assistance, unless you have a rich father or wife! I'm not even talking about Olympic medallists, but average internationals needing nothing more than to break even. Of course there are some internationals such as Dwight Stones and Guy Drut who have admitted to making large sums, even as amateurs. But solely professional athletics is not on either, there must be a mixture of both, in open sport, so that the pros, or those accepting money, are always being challenged, and replaced, by those from below in the normal way as in tennis, say.

The same athletes cannot compete over, say, 5,000 metres every few days, or with the frequency which promoters would be looking for. If you see people running too frequently, then it *must* be a con, because what is happening out there on the track cannot be genuine. There are lots of athletes around at the present moment who are not running flat out at the big sponsored international meetings, either because they are tired or saving themselves. I have never yet run in a race where I was not giving absolutely my best and attempting to win. What is needed in Open athletics is prize money rather than appearance money, because prize money guarantees a commitment. But the prize money should be graded down to tenth place or so, because you need a field to make a race and someone has to come last. A lot of the sting has been taken out of the present problems by the International Federation relaxing the regulations on advertising and endorsements, which is how sportsmen like Borg and Ballesteros make so much of their money. As people know, I have now made a commercial for Horlicks.

But there *must* be free interplay between the amateur and the pro in athletics; under no circumstances should those who want to run for fun, or who are not good enough to command a fee, be frozen out. The youngsters on the way up need the experience against the top competitors in order to develop, just as I did when I was eighteen or nineteen, and was able to race against Walker, Quax, Dixon and Bayi. Only in that way was I able to develop into an international athlete. It is bad to have a situation, as in professional snooker, where the pros control who gets a professional licence, because they don't want an unknown coming in and sweeping the table. Nor must we ever allow athletics to get like boxing, where managers and promoters control who gets to the top, who gets the fights. The only reason you should be able to run in an Olympic or World Championship 1,500 metres final is because you are good enough to be there. But in the present sham-amateur world it's difficult to get to the top without getting caught up in the twilight area of ducking and diving; it obliges honest people to become dishonest. I've been fortunate initially to have tremendous support from my parents, and latterly sponsorship from the Sports Aid Foundation and Otis, who helped to make possible my preparation for the Olympics.

The importance of my gold medal in Moscow was not just my own pride, but the position of influence I hope it gives me to help shape athletics, to prevent it becoming a promoter's and sponsor's carve-up, to keep it open for young people coming up so that they can get races without being told when, where and even *how* they must run. If you become famous it gives you an obligation. You don't ask to be famous (though perhaps some do), but if you are then you should accept the burden which goes with it, as Mary Peters has done in Belfast. The power to influence is enormous and it has to be used the right way. We do not want a generation of young athletes who think it is smart to come waving down the finishing straight as we saw in the 1980 English Schools championships. I don't feel like leaving the sport and turning it over to some of the people who are in it at the moment. There is a misguided battle going on between officials wanting to preserve old fashioned amateurism on the one hand, which can only ultimately hasten the commercial take-over, and those who are not in the race to win but to see who can make the first million, on the other.

It is inevitable that athletics *will* go Open, but it is vital that it does not just become a licence to print money for the leading competitors and a handful of promoters and advertising agents, collaborating with television, and important that the IAAF retains some sort of control. All of us at the top, including Ovett, Thompson, and Wells, ought to be thinking very carefully not only of ourselves, but of what sort of sport we want to hand on to the next generation. It is vital that the young runners of enormous potential which Britain possesses just below the highest level, such as Dave Warren, Steve Cram, Graham Williamson, Gary Oakes, and Chris McGeorge and all those coming through behind them, should be free to develop in the races and over the distances they need, without being required to accommodate the demands of promoters and sponsors. Of course sponsors have to receive value for money, but sport has to remain sport, a concept rooted on the track and not in the balance sheet. It must not become another consumer-entertainment package. In all sports we have to protect the fundamentals of sportsmanship, self-determination of the individual and the pursuit of excellence free of commercial expediency, and as Voltaire said, 'the price of freedom is eternal vigilance'. ❯

Back on the track, speculation continued throughout the winter of 1981-82 about an eventual confrontation with Ovett other than in, possibly, the 1982 European Championship in Athens.

‘ The first suitable time for both of us was always likely to be an AAA or British Board meeting in mid-summer. We both approach the season differently. For instance, I don't do Steve's high mileage, but start the season with more speed work. Obviously, though, the interest in a meeting is over a mile or 1,500 metres, though I still regard myself at present as much as an 800 metres runner as a miler. A series of three races was projected between us: an 800, a 1,500 and a mile would seem to be the fairest solution. Yet my main objective for 1982 is to win the European 800 metres and 1,500 metres, if I can. My winter training is geared to coping with both races in both European and Commonwealth Games.

After that I think I will definitely move up to the 5,000 metres for the inaugural World Championships in Helsinki in 1983. The 5,000 is one of the great races of the track. It's twelve-and-a-half laps, and about thirteen minutes is a nice time to be on the track, for the crowd to get involved. With 1,500 metres the tactics are more limited, the 5,000 offers greater flexibility. I don't think anybody could run me out in the first mile, or the last mile, so therefore the grey area is the four-and-a-half laps in the middle. At present, a long run for home in the 5,000 is thought of as the last two laps. Why not the last three?

I will retire after the World Championships, or the Olympics in 1984, because by then I will have spent enough time concentrating severely on one thing, and even then it might have been too long. If I'd been twenty-six in Moscow instead of twenty-three, I would have retired then. I realize that when I stop, I run the risk of feeling unfulfilled, that I will miss the exhilaration of competition. One can get to a point where you need to feel extended almost to the point of breaking, but I will not want to linger on.

For the moment I can still put up with the life, the training – it's endurable, it's combined with so many other things. I don't understand why, but I'm getting more enjoyment than ever from running. Mentally I'm harder, I can push myself when I need to, but when the season finishes, it finishes. The training goes on, but I never read athletics magazines or papers. There is no doubt that the Olympics did free me. The real motivation now, far more than medals or records, is the satisfaction of the continuing experiment with Peter, the endless quest for improvement. Perfection is always just around the corner. ’

APPENDIX A

A complete list of the track races in which Sebastian Coe has competed since 1973, when he was sixteen

Abbreviations

pb-personal best   sf-semi final   UK-United Kingdom record
  h -heat   cr-championship record   WR-World record
  f -final   CR-Commonwealth record   *-on cinders

Date	Event	Track	Distance	Place	Time
1973					
17 March	UK Indoor Championships	Cosford	800 m	4th	2:2.5
1 May	B. Milers' Club	Stretford	800 m	3rd	1:56.6
5 May	Longwood Youth	Huddersfield	1,500 m	1st	4:7.4
13 May	B. Milers' Club	Crystal Palace	800 m	2nd	1:56.0(pb)
18 May	West District Schools	Sheffield	800 m	1st	2:1.1
18 May	West District Schools	Sheffield	1,500 m	1st	4:15.4
23 May	Sheffield Selection	Sheffield	3,000 m	1st	8:43.7
3 June	Northern League	Sheffield	1,500 m	3rd	4:7.5
9 June	Yorks Schools Championships	York	3,000 m	1st	8:49.0
16 June	N. Counties	Sheffield	1,500 m	3rd	3:59.5(pb)
7 July	English Schools	Bebington	3,000 m	1st	8:40.2 (pb)
17 July	S. Yorks League	Doncaster	800 m	1st	1:59.7
21 July	City Championships	Sheffield	800 m	1st	1:57.0
21 July	City Championships	Sheffield	1,500 m	1st	4:7.4
4 Aug	AAA Youth Championships	Aldersley	1,500 m	1st	3:55.0 (pb)
14 Aug	Stretford League	Manchester	3,000 m	6th	8:34.6 (pb)
9 Sept	Hallam Harriers Championships	Sheffield	400 m		51.8 (pb)
15 Sept	Rotherham Festival	Rotherham	1,500 m	1st	3:58.0
1974					
10 April	Training run	Rotherham	800 m		1:55.1 (pb)
April-Nov	Injured with stress fractures				
1975					
21 March	Indoor Under 20 Championships	Cosford	1,500 m (h)	2nd	4:8.0
22 March	Indoor Under 20 Championships	Cosford	1,500 m (f)	1st	3:54.4 (pb)
13 April	Pye Cup	Cleckheaton	1,500 m	1st	3:49.7 (pb)

Date	Event	Track	Distance	Place	Time
30 April	B. Milers' Club	Rawtenstall	1,500 m	1st	3:54.0
31 May	Yorks Senior Championships	Cleckheaton	1,500 m	1st	3:51.3
8 June	Pye Cup	Cleckheaton	800 m	1st	1:53.8 (pb)
8 June	Pye Cup	Cleckheaton	4 × 400 m		50.5
21 June	N. Counties Under 20	Gateshead	1,500 m	1st	3:50.8
25 June	Northern League	Sheffield	300 m	2nd	36.2 (pb)
28 June	N. Counties Under 20	Blackburn	3,000 m	1st	8:14.2 (pb)
26 July	AAA Junior Championships	Kirkby	1,500 (h)	1st	3:52.0
27 July	AAA Junior Championships	Kirkby	1,500 m (f)	1st	3:49.1 (pb)
30 July	GB v France/Spain	Warley	1,500 m	1st	3:50.3
23 Aug	European Junior Ch'ships	Athens	1,500 m (h)		3.48.0 (pb)
24 Aug	European Junior Ch'ships	Athens	1,500 m (f)	3rd	3:45.2 (pb)

1976

Date	Event	Track	Distance	Place	Time
24 Jan	UK Indoor Championships	Cosford	1,500 m	5th	3:51.0
6 March	Loughborough Match	Crystal Palace	4 × 800 m		1:52.0 (pb)
20 March	Loughborough Match	Cosford	600 relay/leg		80.4 (pb)
28 March	B. Milers' Club	Stretford	1,500 m	1st	3:47.4
14 April	H. Wilson Mile	Crystal Palace	1 mile	1st	4:7.6
1 May	B. Milers' Club	Stretford	1 mile	1st	4:5.7 (pb)
12 May	Loughborough Match	Loughborough	800 m	1st	1:53.0
16 May	Yorkshire Championships	Cleckheaton	1,500 m	1st	3:43.3 (pb)
19 May	Loughborough v Borough Rd	Isleworth	800 m	1st	1:53.0
31 May	Inter-Counties Championships	Crystal Palace	1 mile	2nd	4:2.4 (pb)
11 June	Olympic Selection	Crystal Palace	1,500 m	7th	3:43.2 (pb)
17 June	Loughborough v AAA	Loughborough	800 m	1st	1:50.7 (pb)
24 July	Heckington Sports	Heckington	1 mile	1st	4:9.1
1 Aug	Open Meeting	Nottingham	1,000 m	1st	2:30.0
8 Aug	B. Milers' Club	Stretford	800 m	1st	1:47.7 (pb)
13 Aug	AAA Championships	Crystal Palace	1,500 m (h)	3rd	3:45.05
14 Aug	AAA Championships	Crystal Palace	1,500 m (f)	4th	3:42.6 (pb)
21 Aug	Rediffusion Games	Gateshead	1 mile	3rd	4:1.7 (pb)
30 Aug	Emsley Carr Mile	Crystal Palace	1 mile	7th	3:58.3 (pb)
14 Sept	Bell's Games	Gateshead	1 mile	2nd	4:0.5

1977

Date	Event	Track	Distance	Place	Time
29 Jan	UK Indoor Championships	Cosford	800 m	1st	1:49.1 (pb/cr)
19 Feb	GB v W. Germany	Dortmund	800 m	1st	1:47.6 (CR)

Date	Event	Track	Distance	Place	Time
26 Feb	GB v France	Cosford	800 m	1st	1:47.5 (CR)
12 March	European Indoor Ch'ships	San Sebastian	800 m (h)	1st	1:50.5
13 March	European Indoor Ch'ships	San Sebastian	800 m (sf)	1st	1:48.25
14 March	European Indoor Ch'ships	San Sebastian	800 m (f)	1st	1:46.54 (CR)
3 July	Dewhurst Games	Spalding	800 m	1st	1:51.7
23 July	AAA Championships	Crystal Palace	800 m	2nd	1:46.8 (pb)
30 July	Philips Games	Gateshead	800 m	2nd	1:47.4
14 Aug	Europa Cup	Helsinki	800 m	4th	1:47.6
16 Aug	Ivo Van Damme	Brussels	800 m	3rd	1:46.3 (pb)
24 Aug	Club Meeting	Rotherham	400 m	1st	49.1
28 Aug	GB v W. Germany	Crystal Palace	800 m	1st	1:47.8
29 Aug	Emsley Carr Mile	Crystal Palace	1 mile	1st	3:57.7 (pb)
7 Sept	Courage Games	St Ives	800 m	1st	1:48.1
9 Sept	Coca-Cola	Crystal Palace	800 m	2nd	1:44.95 (UK)

1978

Date	Event	Track	Distance	Place	Time
26 April	Loughborough Match	Loughborough	400 m	1st	48.0 (pb)
10 May	Loughborough Match	Isleworth	400 m	1st	47.7 (pb)
14 May	Yorkshire Championships	Cleckheaton	800 m	1st	1:45.6 (CR)
1 June	Loughborough v AAA	Loughborough	800 m	1st	1:50.0
9 July	Philips Games	Gateshead	800 m	1st	1:46.8
15 July	UK Championships	Meadowbank	800 m	1st	1:47.1
9 Aug	International Invitation	Viareggio	800 m	1st	1:45.7
18 Aug	Ivo Van Damme	Brussels	800 m	1st	1:44.26 (UK)
31 Aug	European Championships	Prague	800 m	3rd	1:44.8
15 Sept	Coca-Cola	Crystal Palace	800 m	1st	1:43.97 (UK)
17 Sept	McEwans Games	Gateshead	1 mile	1st	4:2.2

1979

Date	Event	Track	Distance	Place	Time
27 Jan	UK Indoor Championships	Cosford	3,000 m	1st	7:59.8
25 April	Loughborough Match	Crystal Palace	400 m	2nd	48.3
20 May	Yorkshire Championships	Cleckheaton	800 m	1st	1:50.5
21 May	Yorkshire Championships	Cleckheaton	400 m	1st	47.6 (pb)
23 May	Loughborough Match	Loughborough	400 m	1st	47.4 (pb)
23 May	Loughborough Match	Loughborough	800 m	1st	1:54.8
31 May	Loughborough v AAA	Loughborough	800 m	1st	1:47.8
16 June	N. Counties Championships	Costeloe Park	800 m	1st	1:46.3
30 June	Europa Cup	Malmo	800 m (sf)	1st	1:46.63

178

Date	Event	Track	Distance	Place	Time
3 July	Bislet Games	Oslo	800 m	1st	1:42.33 (WR)
14 July	AAA Championships	Crystal Palace	400 m	2nd	46.85 (pb)
17 July	Golden Mile	Oslo	1 mile	1st	3:48.95 (WR)
5 Aug	International Invitation	Viareggio	800 m	1st	1:50.0
8 Aug	Europa Cup	Turin	800 m (f)	1st	1:47.3
15 Aug	Weltklasse	Zürich	1,500 m	1st	3:32.03 (WR)

1980

Date	Event	Track	Distance	Place	Time
26 April	Loughborough Match	Crystal Palace	3,000 m	1st	7:57.4
7 May	Loughborough Match	Isleworth	1,500 m	1st	3:45.1
11 May	Yorkshire Championships	Cudworth	5,000 m	1st	14:6.0
21 May	England v Belgium	Crystal Palace	800 m	1st	1:47.5
25 May	Inter-Counties Championships	Birmingham	800 m (h)	1st	1:49.0
26 May	Inter-Counties Championships	Birmingham	800 m (f)	1st	1:45.41
1 June	International Invitation	Turin	800 m	1st	1:45.8
5 June	Loughborough v AAA	Loughborough	800 m	1st	1:44.98 (WR)°
7 June	N. Counties	Cleckheaton	800 m	1st	1:44.7
14 June	UK Championships	Crystal Palace	400 m	2nd	47.0
1 July	Bislet Games	Oslo	1,000 m	1st	2:13.4(WR)
24 July	Olympic Games	Moscow	800 m (h)	1st	1:48.5
25 July	Olympic Games	Moscow	800 m (sf)	1st	1:46.7
26 July	Olympic Games	Moscow	800 m (f)	2nd	1:45.9
30 July	Olympic Games	Moscow	1,500 m (h)	2nd	3:40.1
31 July	Olympic Games	Moscow	1,500 m (sf)	1st	3:39.4
1 Aug	Olympic Games	Moscow	1,500 m (f)	1st	3:38.4
8 Aug	Coca-Cola	Crystal Palace	800 m	1st	1:45.0
13 Aug	Weltklasse	Zürich	1,500 m	1st	3:32.19
14 Aug	International Invitation	Viareggio	800 m	2nd	1:45.01

1981

Date	Event	Track	Distance	Place	Time
24 Jan	AAA Indoor Championships	Cosford	3,000 m	1st	7:55.2
11 Feb	GB v GDR (Indoor)	Cosford	800 m	1st	1:46.0 (WR)
3 May	UAU Championships	Crystal Palace	400 m	1st	46.9
13 May	Loughborough Match	Borough Road	400 m	1st	47.4
17 May	Yorkshire Championships	Cleckheaton	800 m	1st	1:46.3
3 June	England v USA/Eth/Bel	Crystal Palace	800 m	1st	1:44.06
3 June	England v USA/Eth/Bel	Crystal Palace	4 × 400		45.7
7 June	GB v USSR	Gateshead	4 × 400		46.5

Date	Event	Track	Distance	Place	Time
10 June	International Invitation	Florence	800 m	1st	1:41.72 (WR)
5 July	Europa Cup	Helsinki	800 m	1st	1:47.57
7 July	International Invitation	Stockholm	1,500 m	1st	3:31.95 (pb)
11 July	Bislet Games	Oslo	1,000 m	1st	2:12.18 (WR)
17 July	GB v USSR	Gateshead	800 m	1st	1:47.4
19 July	Dairygate	Leicester	1,000 m	1st	2:17.4
31 July	Talbot Games	Crystal Palace	800 m	1st	1:46.67
5 Aug	International Invitation	Viareggio	800 m	1st	1:47.12
7 Aug	AAA Championships	Crystal Palace	800 m (sf)	1st	1:45.89
8 Aug	AAA Championships	Crystal Palace	800 m (f)	1st	1:45.45
15 Aug	Europa Cup	Zagreb	800 m	1st	1:47.03
19 Aug	International Invitation	Zürich	1 mile	1st	3:48.53 (WR)
28 Aug	Golden Mile	Brussels	1 mile	1st	3:47.33 (WR)
4 Sept	World Cup	Rome	800 m	1st	1:46.18

APPENDIX B

Evolution of World Records
800 metres

Time	Runner	Nation	Date	Place
1:51.9	Ted Meredith	USA	8.7.1912	Stockholm
1:51.6	Otto Peltzer	Germany	3.7.1926	London
1:50.6	Séra Martin	France	14.7.1928	Paris
1:49.8	Tom Hampson	GB	2.8.1932	Los Angeles
1:49.8	Ben Eastman	USA	16.6.1934	Princeton
1:49.7	Glenn Cunningham	USA	20.8.1936	Stockholm
1:49.6	Elroy Robinson	USA	11.7.1937	New York
1:48.4	Sydney Wooderson	GB	20.8.1938	Motspur Park
1:46.6	Rudolf Harbig	Germany	15.7.1939	Milan
1:45.7	Roger Moens	Belgium	3.8.1955	Oslo
1:44.3	Peter Snell	New Zealand	3.2.1962	Christchurch
1:44.3	Ralph Doubell	Australia	15.10.1968	Mexico City
1:44.3	Dave Wottle	USA	1.7.1972	Eugene
1:43.7	Marcello Fiasconaro	Italy	27.6.1973	Milan
1:43.5	Alberto Juantorena	Cuba	25.7.1976	Montreal
1:43.44	Alberto Juantorena	Cuba	21.8.1977	Sofia
1:42.33	Sebastian Coe	GB	3.7.1979	Oslo
1:41.72	Sebastian Coe	GB	10.6.1981	Florence

1,000 metres

Time	Runner	Nation	Date	Place
2:32.3	Georg Mickler	Germany	22.6.1913	Hanover
2.29.1	Anatole Bolin	Sweden	22.9.1918	Stockholm
2.28.6	Sven Lundgren	Sweden	27.9.1922	Stockholm
2:26.8	Séra Martin	France	30.9.1926	Paris
2:25.8	Otto Peltzer	Germany	18.9.1927	Paris
2:23.6	Jules Ladoumègue	France	19.10.1930	Paris
2:21.5	Rudolf Harbig	Germany	24.5.1941	Dresden
2:21.4	Rune Gustafsson	Sweden	4.9.1946	Borås
2:21.4	Marcel Hansenne	France	27.8.1948	Gothenburg
2:21.3	Olle Åberg	Sweden	10.8.1952	Copenhagen

Time	Runner	Nation	Date	Place
2:21.2	Stanislav Jungwirth	Czechoslovakia	27.10.1952	Stará Boleslav
2:20.8	Mal Whitfield	USA	16.8.1953	Eskilstuna
2:20.4	Audun Boysen	Norway	17.9.1953	Oslo
2:19.5	Audun Boysen	Norway	18.8.1954	Gävle
2:19.0	Audun Boysen	Norway	30.8.1955	Gothenburg
2:19.0	István Rózsavölgyi	Hungary	21.9.1955	Tata
2:18.1	Dan Waern	Sweden	19.9.1958	Turku
2:17.8	Dan Waern	Sweden	21.8.1959	Karlstad
2:16.7	Siegfried Valentin	GDR	19.7.1960	Potsdam
2:16.6	Peter Snell	New Zealand	12.11.1964	Auckland
2:16.2	Jürgen May	GDR	20.7.1965	Erfurt
2:16.2	Franz-Josef Kemper	Germany	21.9.1966	Hanover
2:16.0	Daniel Malan	South Africa	24.6.1973	Munich
2:13.9	Rick Wohlhuter	USA	30.7.1974	Oslo
2:13.4	Sebastian Coe	GB	1.7.1980	Oslo
2:12.18	Sebastian Coe	GB	11.7.1981	Oslo

1,500 metres

Time	Runner	Nation	Date	Place
3:55.8	Abel Kiviat	USA	8.6.1912	Cambridge, Mass
3.54.7	John Zander	Sweden	5.8.1917	Stockholm
3:52.6	Paavo Nurmi	Finland	19.6.1924	Helsinki
3:51.0	Otto Peltzer	Germany	11.9.1926	Berlin
3:49.2	Jules Ladoumègue	France	5.10.1930	Paris
3:49.2	Luigi Beccali	Italy	9.9.1933	Turin
3:49.0	Luigi Beccali	Italy	17.9.1933	Milan
3:48.8	Bill Bonthron	USA	30.6.1934	Milwaukee
3:47.8	Jack Lovelock	New Zealand	6.8.1936	Berlin
3:47.6	Gunder Hägg	Sweden	10.8.1941	Stockholm
3:45.8	Gunder Hägg	Sweden	17.7.1942	Stockholm
3:45.0	Arne Andersson	Sweden	17.8.1943	Gothenburg
3:43.0	Gunder Hägg	Sweden	7.7.1944	Gothenburg
3:43.0	Lennart Strand	Sweden	15.7.1947	Malmö
3:43.0	Werner Lueg	Germany	29.6.1952	Berlin
3:42.8	Wes Santee	USA	4.6.1954	Compton
3:41.8	John Landy	Australia	21.6.1954	Turku

Time	Runner	Nation	Date	Place
3:40.8	Sándor Iharos	Hungary	28.7.1955	Helsinki
3:40.8	Lásló Tábori	Hungary	6.9.1955	Oslo
3:40.8	Gunnar Nielson	Denmark	6.9.1955	Oslo
3:40.6	István Rózsavölgyi	Hungary	3.8.1956	Tata
3:40.2	Olavi Salsola	Finland	11.7.1957	Turku
3:40.2	Olavi Salonen	Finland	11.7.1957	Turku
3:38.1	Stanislav Jungwirth	Czechoslovakia	12.7.1957	Stará Boleslav
3:36.0	Herb Elliott	Australia	28.8.1958	Gothenburg
3:35.6	Herb Elliott	Australia	6.9.1960	Rome
3:33.1	Jim Ryun	USA	8.7.1967	Los Angeles
3:32.2	Filbert Bayi	Tanzania	2.2.1974	Christchurch
3:32.1	Sebastian Coe	GB	15.8.1979	Oslo
3:31.4	Steve Ovett	GB	27.8.1980	Koblenz

1 mile

Time	Runner	Nation	Date	Place
4:14.4	John Paul Jones	USA	31.5.1913	Cambridge, Mass
4:12.6	Norman Taber	USA	16.7.1915	Cambridge, Mass
4:10.4	Paavo Nurmi	Finland	23.8.1923	Stockholm
4:09.2	Jules Ladoumègue	France	4.10.1931	Paris
4:07.6	Jack Lovelock	New Zealand	15.7.1933	Princeton
4:06.8	Glenn Cunningham	USA	16.6.1934	Princeton
4:06.4	Sydney Wooderson	GB	28.8.1937	Motspur Park
4:06.2	Gunder Hägg	Sweden	1.7.1942	Gothenburg
4:06.2	Arne Andersson	Sweden	10.7.1942	Stockholm
4:04.6	Gunder Hägg	Sweden	4.9.1942	Stockholm
4:02.6	Arne Andersson	Sweden	1.7.1943	Gothenburg
4:01.6	Arne Andersson	Sweden	18.7.1944	Malmö
4:01.4	Gunder Hägg	Sweden	17.7.1945	Malmö
3:59.4	Roger Bannister	GB	6.5.1954	Oxford
3:58.0	John Landy	Australia	21.6.1954	Turku
3:57.2	Derek Ibbotson	GB	19.7.1957	London
3:54.5	Herb Elliott	Australia	6.8.1958	Dublin
3:54.4	Peter Snell	New Zealand	27.1.1962	Wanganui
3:54.1	Peter Snell	New Zealand	17.11.1964	Auckland
3:53.6	Michel Jazy	France	9.6.1965	Rennes

Time	Runner	Nation	Date	Place
3:51.3	Jim Ryun	USA	17.7.1966	Berkeley
3:51.1	Jim Ryun	USA	23.6.1967	Bakersfield
3:51.0	Filbert Bayi	Tanzania	17.5.1975	Kingston
3:49.4	John Walker	New Zealand	12.8.1975	Gothenburg
3:49.0	Sebastian Coe	GB	17.7.1979	Oslo
3:48.8	Steve Ovett	GB	1.7.1980	Oslo
3:48.53	Sebastian Coe	GB	19.8.1981	Zürich
3:48.40	Steve Ovett	GB	26.8.1981	Koblenz
3:47.33	Sebastian Coe	GB	28.8.1981	Brussels

Appendix C

World Record Split-Times (with the times between each given distance in brackets)

1,500 metres

	400 m	800 m	1,000 m	1,200 m	1,500 m
Zander (1917)	59.0	2:02.0(63.0)		3:07.5(65.5)	3:54.7 (47.2)
Nurmi (1924)	57.3	2:01.0(63.7)	2:33.0	3:06.0(65.0)	3:52.6(46.6)
Peltzer (1926)	61.5	2:03.0(61.5)	2:35.0	3:06.0(63.0)	3:51.0(45.0)
Ladoumègue (1930)	58.8	2:00.6(61.8)	2:33.0	3:05.0(64.4)	3:49.2(44.2)
Beccali (1933)	60.0	1:59.4(59.4)	2:32.8	3:07.0(67.6)	3:49.0(42.0)
Bonthron (1934)	61.0	2:01.2(62.0)		3:06.0(64.8)	3:48.8(42.8)
Lovelock (1936)	61.6	2:05.5(63.9)	2:36.0	3:05.4(59.9)	3:47.8(42.4)
Hägg (1941)	59.0	2:02.1(63.1)	2:33.0	3:03.5(61.4)	3:47.6(44.1)
Andersson (1943)	58.5	2:01.0(62.5)	2:31.0	3:00.8(59.8)	3:45.0(44.2)
Hägg (1944)	56.7	1:56.5(59.8)	2:27.2	2:58.0(61.5)	3:43.0(45.0)
Strand (1947)	57.8	1:59.3(61.5)	2:29.5	2:59.6(60.3)	3:43.0(43.4)
Santee (1954)	57.8	1:58.0(60.2)		2:58.0(60.0)	3:42.8(44.8)
Landy (1954)	57.9	1:57.5(59.6)	2:27.5	2:57.3(59.8)	3:41.8(44.5)
Salsola (1957)	56.8	1:57.8(61.0)	2:28.0	2:58.4(60.6)	3:40.2(41.8)
Jungwirth (1957)	54.9	1:54.2(59.3)	2:24.2	2:53.4(59.2)	3:38.1(44.7)
Elliott (1958)	57.5	1:57.5(60.0)	2:28.0	2:55.5(58.0)	3:36.0(40.5)
Elliott (1960)	58.5	1:58.2(59.3)	2:25.4	2:54.1(55.9)	3:35.6(41.5)
Ryun (1967)	60.5	1:56.0(55.5)	2:25.2	2:53.5(57.5)	3:33.1(39.6)
Bayi (1974)	54.9	1:52.2(57.3)	2:21.0	2:50.2(58.0)	3:32.2(42.0)
Coe (1979)	54.4	1:53.2(58.8)		2:49.5(56.3)	3:32.1(42.6)
Ovett (1980)	55.5	1:53.0(57.5)		2:50.7(57.7)	3:31.4(40.7)

One Mile

	¼ mile	½ mile	¾ mile	1,500 m	1 mile
Lang (1865)	60.0	2:05.5(65.5)	3:14.0(68.5)		4:17.2(63.2)
George (1886)	58.2	2:01.7(63.5)	3:07.7(66.0)		4:12.7(65.0)
Taber (1915)	58.0	2:05.0(67.0)	3:13.0(68.0)	3:55.0	4:12.6(59.6)
Nurmi (1923)	60.3	2:03.2(62.9)	3:06.7(63.5)	3:53.0	4:10.4(63.7)
Ladoumègue (1931)	60.8	2:04.2(63.4)	3:08.0(63.8)	3:52.4	4:09.2(61.2)

	¼ mile	½ mile	1,500m	1 mile
Lovelock (1933)	61.4	2:03.6(62.2)	3:08.7(65.1)		4:07.6(58.9)
Cunningham (1934)	61.8	2:05.8(64.0)	3:07.6(61.8)		4:06.8(59.1)
Wooderson (1937)	58.6	2:02.6(64.0)	3:07.2(64.6)		4:06.4(59.2)
Hägg (1942)	59.1	2:02.0(62.9)	3:05.8(63.8)	3:50.8	4:06.2(60.3)
Hägg (1942)	57.2	2:00.2(63.0)	3:04.2(64.0)		4:04.6(60.4)
Andersson (1943)	59.4	2:00.8(61.4)	3:04.0(63.2)	3:47.4	4:02.6(58.6)
Andersson (1944)	57.1	1:56.8(59.7)	2:59.5(62.7)	3:46.0	4:01.6(62.1)
Hägg (1945)	56.7	1:59.2(62.5)	3:01.4(62.2)	3:45.4	4:01.4(60.0)
Bannister (1954)	57.5	1:58.2(60.7)	3:00.5(62.3)	3:43.0	3:59.4(58.9)
Landy (1954)	58.2	1:58.2(60.0)	2:58.4(60.2)	3:41.8	3:58.0(59.5)
Ibbotson (1957)	56.0	1:56.4(60.4)	3:00.4(64.0)	3:41.9	3:57.2(56.8)
Elliott (1958)	56.4	1:58.0(61.6)	2:59.0(61.0)	3:39.6	3:54.5(55.5)
Snell (1962)	60.7	2:00.6(59.9)	2:59.6(59.0)	3:39.3	3:54.4(54.8)
Snell (1964)	56.0	1:54.0(58.0)	2:54.0(60.0)	3:37.6	3:54.1(60.1)
Jazy (1965)	57.3	1:56.5(59.2)	2:57.4(60.9)	3:38.4	3:53.6(56.2)
Ryun (1967)	57.9	1:55.5(57.6)	2:55.3(59.8)	3:36.1	3:51.1(56.0)
Bayi (1975)	56.9	1:56.6(59.7)	2:55.3(58.7)	3:35.0	3:51.0(55.7)
Walker (1975)	56.3	1:55.5(58.2)	2:53.5(58.0)	3:34.3	3:49.4(55.9)
Coe (1979)	57.8	1:55.3(57.5)	2:53.4(58.1)	3:32.8	3:49.0(55.6)
Ovett (1980)	55.7	1:53.8(58.1)	2:51.0(57.2)	3:32.7	3:48.8(57.8)
Coe (1981)	56.5	1:54.2(57.7)	2:52.6(58.4)	3:33.3	3:48.53(56.0)
Ovett (1981)	56.6	1:54.5(57.9)	2:51.5(57.0)		3:48.40(56.9)
Coe (1981)	55.3	1:53.3(58.0)	2:51.9(58.6)	3:32.93	3:47.33(55.5)

Index

Book Tokens

**Give them
the pleasure of choosing**

Book Tokens can be bought
and exchanged at most
bookshops in Great Britain
and Ireland.